"*Orphanology* presents a gospel-centered theological and practical approach to an often-neglected sphere of ministry. Morton and Merida call Christians to reflect God's image as redeemer, defender, provider, and father, and take up the cause for those who have no voice. It is engaging, thorough, accessible, and a convicting joy to read."

—ED STETZER, COAUTHOR OF *Transformational Church*, www.edstetzer.com

"I wept as I read the great truths in *Orphanology*. Not just because it reminded me of forgotten details in the adoption story of our son Rudy, or because it compelled me to a greater place of action for the nearly 150 million orphans in our world, but more than anything because it ignited worship and thanksgiving for a God who would adopt ME! Orphan me. Abandoned me. Fatherless me. Undeserving me. . . . Thank you, Tony and Rick, for this powerful book."

—DAVID NASSER, PASTOR; AUTHOR OF *A Call to Die*

"*Orphanology* challenges believers to be instrumental in rescuing the weak and fatherless, thus fulfilling the Great Commission! As an adoptive father and pastor, I believe this book has the potential to transform the body of Christ's approach to orphan care and ministry."

—KEVIN EZELL, PRESIDENT, NORTH AMERICAN MISSION BOARD

"*Orphanology* is a clarion call for everyone who calls themselves a believer. It articulately weds together the proclamation of the gospel and the caring for orphans . . . spurring us to envision God-sized ideas for bringing solutions to this crisis. Do good. Read this book."

—ANDY LEHMAN, VICE-PRESIDENT, LIFESONG FOR ORPHANS;
BOARD MEMBER, CHRISTIAN ALLIANCE FOR ORPHANS

"*Orphanology* is another great resource every church that cares about the orphan crisis should have. This book will not only give you good theology about caring for orphans, it will also give much needed practical help."

—JOHNNY CARR, NATIONAL DIRECTOR OF CHURCH PARTNERSHIPS,
BETHANY CHRISTIAN SERVICES

"Brilliant. I cannot imagine that one could read this and remain neutral or disengaged in respect to orphans and the church."

— MICAH FRIES, PASTOR, FREDERICK BOꞮ   ', MISSOURI

"*Orphanology* is an excellent resource for the adoption and orphan care movement. As you read the personal stories recorded in these pages, you'll be moved to tears . . . and then to action."

—TREVIN WAX, AUTHOR OF *Holy Subversion: Allegiance to Christ in an Age of Rivals*

"*Orphanology* is compelling exposition of Scripture wedded to compassionate exhortation. It is my prayer that this book will be a catalyst to engage families and churches for the sake of orphans around the world and across the street!"

—TIM BRISTER, PASTOR, GRACE BAPTIST CHURCH; DIRECTOR, PLNTD NETWORK

"Simple, straightforward, convincing, and convicting. I am thrilled at the renewed interest in orphan care and adoption that is sweeping through the evangelical church. This book reflects this movement, and will stoke the fires of it too! We bless You, Lord, for moving so powerfully among your adopted sons and daughters."

—DANIEL L. AKIN, PRESIDENT, SOUTHEASTERN BAPTIST THEOLOGICAL SEMINARY

"*Orphanology* carries a remarkable blend of depth and breadth, engaging story and substantive theology, big picture vision and practical how-to. It offers both a compelling invitation into orphan care, foster and adoption ministry, as well as dependable guidance along a road that is likely to be as costly and as rewarding as anything you've ever done." —JEDD MEDEFIND, PRESIDENT, CHRISTIAN ALLIANCE FOR ORPHANS AND COAUTHOR OF *UPENDED.*

"*Orphanology* shows us how much God cares about orphans and why we should too. Read this book and then ask this simple question, 'Lord, what do You want me to do?' God's answer may surprise you and change your life forever."

—DR. RAY PRITCHARD, PRESIDENT, KEEP BELIEVING MINISTRIES; AUTHOR OF *The Healing Power of Forgiveness, Stealth Attack,* AND *An Anchor for the Soul*

"Reader beware! As I read, I could not help but see my own past complacency regarding this global issue for what it really is—selfishness. The gospel kills selfishness and cultivates Christ's own compassion and love for the fatherless.

—GEORGE G. ROBINSON, DMISS, ASSISTANT PROFESSOR OF MISSIONS AND EVANGELISM, SOUTHEASTERN BAPTIST THEOLOGICAL SEMINARY

"If even a fraction of the vast population of those who call themselves Christians would practice a little *orphanology*, then the world would notice our being salt and light and more than ever glorify our Father in heaven."

—JASON DUKES, AUTHOR OF *Live Sent*

"Merida and Morton's book is as inspirational as it is informative. This book will lead to transformation of children who will be adopted, loved, and cared for, and also to the transformation of anyone who reads and takes its content seriously." —MARK L. RUSSELL, PhD, AUTHOR OF *The Missional Entrepreneur*

"God loves orphans. I hope this book will be widely read by pastors and other church leaders, couples considering adoption (may their tribe increase!), and any Christian who wants to be a part of what God is doing to lead His church to love all the little children of the world whom Jesus loves." — NATHAN FINN, ASSISTANT PROFESSOR OF CHURCH HISTORY AND BAPTIST STUDIES, SOUTHEASTERN BAPTIST THEOLOGICAL SEMINARY

"Tony Merida and Rick Morton have done the church a huge favor with this book because they have clearly shown that adoption and orphan care are gospel issues and have given us intensely practical ways to move our churches to action. This book has especially impacted me because my mom grew up in an orphanage. For a decade she waited in vain for a father to come for her. This book will help churches everywhere say with their Lord Jesus to millions like my mom around the world, 'I will not leave you as orphans; I will come for you!'" —JONATHAN AKIN, PASTOR, FAIRVIEW CHURCH, LEBANON, TENNESSEE

"This is pure Gospel mission. This book takes missional engagement with orphans beyond a fad and to a practical, working strategy." — J.D. GREEAR, PASTOR, THE SUMMIT CHURCH, AUTHOR OF *GOSPEL: Recovering the Power that Made Christianity Revolutionary*

"Read at your own risk! You are about to discover adoption is more crucial, more feasible, and more of a blessing than you ever imagined. This is not a book that will touch you. It is a book that will change you, and you will be glad that it did.

Pregnancy is not the only way to become an expectant parent. Tony Merida and Rick Morton are going to draw you into the heart of a mighty movement of God and release a river of love you did not know you had." —CHUCK KELLEY, PRESIDENT, NEW ORLEANS BAPTIST THEOLOGICAL SEMINARY

"Rick and Tony have written an important book for the church today. While adoption has increased in popularity over the years, many do not fully understand its biblical and missional aspects. If the church can grasp this, lives will be transformed like no other point in history." —MARK MATLOCK, PRESIDENT, WISDOMWORKS MINISTRIES

ORPHANOLOGY

New Hope® Publishers
P. O. Box 12065
Birmingham, AL 35202-2065
www.newhopepublishers.com
New Hope Publishers is a division of WMU®.

Library of Congress Cataloging-in-Publication Data

Merida, Tony, 1977-
Orphanology : awakening to Gospel-centered adoption and orphan
care / Tony Merida and Rick Morton.
p. cm.
Includes bibliographical references.
ISBN-10: 1-59669-302-9
ISBN-13: 978-1-59669-302-9 (sc)
1. Adoption--Religious aspects--Christianity. 2. Orphans--Care..
I. Morton, Rick, 1968- II. Title. III. Title: Awakening to Gospel-
centered adoption and orphan care.
HV875.26.M47 2011
248.4--dc22
2010053463

ISBN-10: 1-59669-302-9
ISBN-13: 978-1-59669-302-9

N114137 • 0712 • 1M5

Interior-page design: Michel Lê.

ORPHANOLOGY

Awakening to
Gospel-Centered
Adoption and
Orphan Care

Tony Merida | Rick Morton

NEW HOPE
PUBLISHERS
Birmingham, Alabama

To our precious wives,
Kimberly Merida and Denise Morton,

and
to our beloved children:
Nastia, Erick, and Nicholas Morton

and
James, Angela, Jana, Victoria, and Joshua Merida

We are headed to a country
with reportedly more than 5 million
orphans. I'm trying to prepare myself
for the gripping images of abandoned
children, hungry children, lonely
children, disfigured children, unwanted
children. We're taking with us two
duffel bags of shoes to give away at the
orphanage, hoping to provide a little
joy and comfort to some children's
lives. But there's so much more to do.
And my heart breaks for these kids...
And I'm trying to prepare myself...
I haven't slept all week. I haven't been
able to get the thought of his little
smile out of my mind, especially the
picture of him holding up a dry-erase
board with *Merida* written
below his name.

CONTENTS

FOREWORD

DAVID PLATT

*I*t was February 15, and we had just landed in Kazakhstan. We were greeted at the airport by our translator. She directed my wife and me to a taxi, where we all took our seats to ride to the orphanage.

"What kind of work do you do?" our translator asked.

"I'm a pastor," I said.

She responded, "A pastor? Why are you a pastor? Don't you know that there is no such thing as God?"

I replied, "Well, I would beg to differ with you."

Such was the beginning of a long conversation that lasted until we came to the orphanage. Upon arrival, we left our conversation behind to focus on the moment ahead. My wife and I were about to be introduced to our first son, Caleb.

We were ushered into a small room where a nurse in the orphanage met us. She shared all sorts of medical information with us about Caleb.

And then it happened.

A woman rounded the corner with a precious ten-month-old boy in her hands. Words cannot adequately describe the immediate swell of emotions that enveloped the room. The woman handed him to my wife, and then to me, and for the first time Caleb looked into the eyes of a mom and a dad.

The next four weeks were filled with all the work and paperwork needed to make Caleb's adoption official. These days were also filled with a multiplicity of conversations with our translator about the gospel. We explained to her how God, in His inexpressibly holy love, sent His Son to live the life we could not live and die the death we deserve to die so that everyone who trusts in Him can be reconciled to God as His child. We shared how, by God's grace, we had been adopted into His family, to know Him as Father and enjoy Him as friend. We told her that this was the motivation behind our wanting to adopt Caleb. Adoption was an expression in our lives of the gospel in our hearts.

She listened . . . and she watched. Over four weeks, she heard us talk about the gospel, and over four weeks, she watched us live out the gospel (albeit an imperfect demonstration at times!).

And then it happened.

It was our last night in Caleb's city, and as we prepared to board the plane, our translator pulled me aside. "I need to tell you something," she said.

"OK," I replied, "what is it?"

"Last night, I trusted in Jesus to save me from myself and my sins. I believe that He is the Lord." Then she said with excitement, "Now I am a child of God!"

A smile swept across my face. I rejoiced with her, encouraged her, and shared with her some initial steps that she could begin to take as a Christian. Time was short, though, and the plane was ready to leave. So I picked up Caleb, and as my wife and I boarded the plane, we looked back, holding a child in our arms while waving good-bye to a child in His arms.

The gospel and adoption are beautifully woven together by the gracious hand of God. In Christ, God has shown His love to us as our Father. He has reached down His hand of mercy to us in the loneliness of our sin, and He has raised us up as members of His family. Consequently, one of the clearest displays of the gospel in this life is when redeemed men and women extend a hand of mercy to children in need and bring them into their families.

I am grateful for Tony Merida and Rick Morton. Tony and I have been good friends for many years, and the power of the gospel is clear in this man's life, family, and ministry. Rick was there when my wife and I first started contemplating adoption, and I can still remember sitting in the Mortons' home, listening to them share the ups and downs, joys and struggles of adoption.

These two brothers know the gospel, and these two brothers know adoption. I am grateful for the time and energy they have put into making this invaluable book available to us. In the pages ahead, you will find strong biblical foundations, warm personal illustrations, and clear practical exhortations. I am confident that, as you read, you will find yourself continually captivated by the love of the Father in heaven and ultimately compelled to show His love to the fatherless on earth.

— DP

INTRODUCTION

WHAT GOSPEL-CENTERED ADOPTION AND ORPHAN CARE MEAN TO US

RICK MORTON

*L*ike life, this book is a narrative about brokenness and redemption. *Orphanology* focuses on orphans and adoption, but at the center of this book, like all of life, is God's eternal story, the gospel. It's really that simple. Yet in the stir of life we can often lose the simplicity. We can miss the point. We can miss the gospel.

That was me. I was that guy. I was a good guy God had rescued from his sin at a young age. At 11 years old I trusted Christ and began to follow Him. I became part of the church and never left. Adolescence was tough, but I never left the church. I struggled with a call to pastor; it was scary. God was patient. I submitted to God's call, and He led me to a wonderful mate. She was God's gift. All was the way it was supposed to be except, as the months and years passed, there were no children. We really wanted children. We loved kids. Our whole lives were wrapped up around kids. Over a decade in youth ministry we spent lots of time with other people's kids, yet none of our own.

As the years passed we tried everything. I can't count the number of doctor visits and fertility clinic consults. The crazy thing about it all was the unconscious disconnect that continued to linger in our lives. We never realized that our struggle to parent children was a gospel issue. Sure, a great part of our desire to parent was the desire to raise children to know Jesus and to serve Him, but it wasn't about mirroring the Father as an adoptive parent or as the Rescuer of the fatherless. The thought honestly never crossed my mind. Actually, as we came to grips with our infertility, our full understanding of God as an adoptive Dad was still forming.

God had adopted me.

Practically, I was the slowest to come around to the idea of adopting. My questions seemed huge (although they seem so silly today!).

Could I really love an adopted child like my own?

Can we afford an adoption?

How can we be sure the child will be healthy?

What happens when the child wants to meet his or her "real" parents?

Should we tell children they are adopted?

My wife was so insistent, so I prayed and I studied, and I began to see something amazing. The crazy thing was that it had been there all along! God had adopted me.

I had read that many, many times, but I had never truly seen it! The Most High God has adopted me! So, did He love me like His own? Did He tell me that I am adopted? Did He worry about my health or did He provide for my progressive growth in His image? How much did He pay for my redemption? Wow!

My questions started to seem pretty small. During the same time God was drawing us to adopt, He gave me the great gift of meeting and teaching alongside Russ Moore at the Southern Baptist Theological Seminary. We found out that the international adoption process can be an unpredictable roller coaster ride, and I am sure that I was an emotional basket case more than once over the twists and turns in the road. Russ was a source of confidence for me as we waded through the waiting and the paperwork. He and his wife, Maria, had adopted their sons Timothy and Benjamin from Russia about a year earlier, and he was always good for an encouraging word or sincere promise for prayer. I will never forget one conversation in particular. I was lamenting about how hard it was to adopt our son and how long it was taking; Russ looked at me with a smile and said, "Yes, but in this process you will learn things about the heart of God that you might not otherwise know." That was prophetic.

What God has unfolded before us over the last several years has been a great journey of understanding Him, His story, His plan, and His people more. It's not that we have it figured out by any means. It's that we see something of Him a little more clearly.

There is another reason for this book for me. It's not all about adoption. I guess I have always had some level of awareness for orphan ministry. My parents were older than those of my peers. When Dad was a preteen in 1929, the Great Depression hit in the US. His mother was a young widow with four kids under the age of 11. Times were tough, and my grandmother lived true to her steady, practical, German values. At one point, the salary she received from her job working in the office of a local physician, Dr. Ross, could not provide for her family—even with the money my dad and my oldest uncle were contributing from their paper routes and other odd jobs. For a time, my grandmother had to place her two youngest (a son and daughter), into a local Catholic orphanage for them to receive food, clothing, and shelter. These two of my dad's siblings were *social orphans*, and this experience changed them. It also changed my family.

My daddy loved his little sister and his little brother more because of this experience. I could always tell, by the way he talked about them. He always grieved their separation and, although he never talked much about it, the scar was always there. Their youngest brother, Ken, always maintained the role of protector that he learned in the orphanage.

My grandmother was not allowed to see her daughter while she was in the orphanage because she was so young. Grandmother would tell stories of standing by the fence at certain times or choosing odd times and routes to go to work or the market in order to create "chance" encounters to see her baby across the playground fence.

I am still amazed about how openly my aunt talked about this experience over the years. My uncle Ken went to be with Jesus when I was a youngster, long before God had given me the experiences or the thoughts that would have made a real conversation about their time in the orphanage of much good for either of us. And I wonder whether that will even matter to us by the time I see him again in eternity. I suspect that we will both be overwhelmed in the presence of the Father, and it won't matter so much.

What I am fairly sure of is that God's call to care for the fatherless here on earth includes many kids like my aunt and uncle were—social orphans, who still have a living parent but are stuck in an institution in the hands of a bureaucratic machine—and that breaks my heart. Over time, God has used those family reminiscences to heighten my sense of commitment to orphans of all kinds, no matter how they may find themselves orphaned. Thanks, Aunt Arva, for being so transparent! I love you for having been so compassionate and real in all those discussions.

If you are concerned with the more than 147 million orphans across the world who will go to bed tonight wondering who will care for them, please read this book. This is an effort to help reduce the learning curve with regard to what the Bible has to say about orphans, and how the church and individual Christians can live out the gospel by ministering to the fatherless. I hope these words not only will remind you of God's command to care for the fatherless, but will challenge you to become involved personally on behalf of the fatherless while giving you practical answers and outlets to begin.

— RM

TONY MERIDA

I just received some thrilling news about 30 minutes ago. My wife texted me saying that we passed our court hearing in Ethiopia for the adoption of our fifth child. We are overjoyed with the anticipation of loving this little guy; teaching him the Scriptures; equipping him to live a full life; and watching this 45-pound six-year-old grow up!

Our newest son's parents died of an illness and he has no brothers and sisters. That's all about to change through the wonder of adoption. Soon, he will have one Ukrainian brother and three Ukrainian sisters. He will also have five Ethiopian cousins.

I never dreamed that we would fill up a minivan with five children. I certainly never dreamed that I would be writing this book on adoption and orphan care. That is, not as of about five years ago. Like Rick, the act of caring for the fatherless through mercy ministry and adoption is a new focus in my life. I was never against adoption. But I had never really considered it seriously until about 2007.

After observing the adoptions of both my sister's and other friends' kids, coupled with my study of the doctrine of adoption and ministry to the fatherless in the Bible, my heart began to burn. Adoption and orphan care became a serious burden. I repented of my lack of participation in caring for the millions of orphans and began praying about what I could do. Soon, my wife and I were looking for an adoption agency, choosing a country, considering how to pay for it, and beginning the process of bringing home some children.

As I travel around the world speaking at various events, I typically talk about adoption and orphan care whenever it's fitting. After initially speaking a few times on the biblical foundations of orphan care and adoption, and sharing our adoption story with others (you'll read this in chapter 1), I kept getting questions. Questions about practical matters such as funding, orphan hosting, foster care, how to lead a church to do orphan care, and more. I sensed that Rick and I should write a book to help expound on these subjects with grace and clarity. We don't claim to be experts; rather pastoral advocates for the fatherless who want to address the questions and provide some of the answers we are experiencing. Each chapter looks at a key question we've asked ourselves and others have asked us.

Of course, this is not simply a book about bringing home the fatherless or about providing food and shelter for them. It's about the gospel. If there is a running theme through *Orphanology*, it's that Rick and I are calling for an awakening to the key answer for reaching the world's orphans: gospel-centered adoption and orphan care.

We are not mere humanitarians. We are leaders in the church who have been changed by Jesus Christ. Everything that we talk about in this book is a reflection on the gospel. Every challenge that we state is motivated by the gospel. Adoption is a real-life illustration of the gospel. It shows us how God transforms spiritual orphans into family members. He changes our names, identities, and families by His grace. Orphan care is acts of mercy that flow from the heart of one who has been changed by the gospel. So, as you read this book, my prayer is that you would love the gospel more deeply and out of that reflection, go display God's Fatherly mercy to a world in need.

$-$ TM

The deepest and strongest
foundation for adoption is located
not in the act of humans adopting
humans, but in God adopting
humans.
And this act is not part of his ordinary
providence in the world;
it is at the heart of the Gospel.

John Piper, "Adoption: The Heart of the Gospel"

1

HOW IS GOD'S ADOPTION OF US SIMILAR TO OUR ADOPTION OF CHILDREN?

*O*ur prayer as we begin this journey together is for you to experience 1 John 3:1, *"See what kind of love the Father has given to us, that we should be called children of God; and so we are."* And if you are a Christian already, please consider afresh God the Father's personal, particular, and persevering love for you, His adopted child. May your consideration of this love God gives create in you a desire to reflect His love to orphans.

Whether you adopt, support those who adopt, or choose from the many other ways to minister to orphans that are discussed in this book, we ask God to use these stories and principles to awaken in you His will concerning these children's lives.

OUR ADOPTION OF CHILDREN

*M*y wife and I began our adoption journey in 2007. Our first real desire for adoption began when my sister (Lisa Bond, whose family's story is in this chapter) brought home two boys from Ethiopia, Beniam (who was four) and Derara (who was seven). I remember us anxiously going home to Kentucky to meet them. My sister already had a biological child whom we loved deeply. But we wondered how these boys would respond to us. As soon as we met them, our hearts melted. We love these boys and miss seeing them regularly. (Later my sister would adopt three more after finding out about Derara's three other siblings).

A burden for orphans often develops by simple exposure to them. If you hold an orphan or visit an orphan, or watch an adopted child grow up in a loving family, then I believe your heart will be moved with compassion. Kimberly and I had witnessed the grace of adoption in some of our friends' lives prior to my sister's journey, as well, but this close familial connection had a deep impact on us.

The second step of our journey occurred shortly after interacting with my sister's children. I came home one day and said, "Baby, I want some kids."

Kimberly said, "Where from?"

I said, "I don't care. Let's fill the house with children." (I must confess that I selfishly wanted to adopt from the Dominican Republic or Haiti because of the number of middle infielders in the major leagues, but my wife insisted that this wasn't good motivation!)

In addition to our initial questions and discussions, that year we were serving at a summer camp and our assignment was to teach on James 1:27 and other texts that dealt with the poor and needy. The study of theses passages together with our personal experience and new awareness of the plight of orphans radically affected us. We began looking at adoption agencies, and then settled on a wonderful Christian agency that worked with a few selected countries. One of these countries was Ukraine. I had a history with Ukraine already. I had taught at a seminary there a few times, and fell in love with the people. My friend Rick had also adopted his son Erick, whom we had grown to love, from Ukraine. So we began the paperwork.

After a lengthy process, 18 months later, the phone finally rang. We thought we would travel in the summer, but we were told that we had to be in Ukraine in a few days, on April 8, 2009. I went to the office, gave my sermon notes to Rick, found two plane tickets, packed, grabbed some stuff for infants, and set out to adopt children. Our paperwork, or dossier, reflected an approval for up to two children, aged five or under. We had dreams of bringing home two little ones.

When we arrived to look at possible children for adoption, we were very tense. We only had about an hour, as people were in line behind us. I can't possibly tell you the emotions that were welling up inside of us. This day was about to set off a chain reaction that would affect many lives for years.

We expected to see pictures of hundreds of kids. Instead, we looked over only a few options, which never felt good for one reason or the other. Then the worker said, "How about three?" So they showed us a sibling group of three, one of them was 14, which didn't feel right. Then, from the other room, another worker passed through our meeting, apparently finished talking to another prospective couple, with about ten minutes or so left, and asked, "How about four?" I looked at Kimberly and said, "Why not?" I've always wanted a lot of kids. I just didn't think we would get them all at once!

When they set before us pictures of four children, all siblings, I looked at them for a second, sat back, and said, "Yes." I then looked at Kimberly, who nervously grinned, and said, "Yes!" Four children, not two children, who were ages 4, 6, 7, and 9! We had been married five years, and were about to have a 9-year-old!

I called my sister to ask her if we were crazy!? I needed someone to tell me no, and she was the one person that I knew would say, "Go for it." She preached me the following sermon:

Sorry I missed your call; I was getting ready for work. Mom called me yesterday morning when I was getting ready and told me about the kids. She was super excited. I was shocked. Honestly, I thought you'd go over and get one baby and come home. LOL. So, when she told me, I cried off ALL my makeup and had to get ready all over again. (I'll get you back for that!)

As to the question of if you are crazy . . . yes, you are. But so was God to send His Son. So was God to forgive us, to adopt us. So was Jesus to be murdered and homeless and penniless. . . . By living out a reckless faith, you are more Christ like than ever before. . . . And, of course, you will be giving a mom and a dad to four older children who otherwise might not ever get one.

Then she quoted Mother Teresa's question and answer to me: *"How can there be too many children? It's like saying there are too many flowers."*

That's all I needed to hear.

Two days later, Kimberly and I journeyed about eight hours south with our local facilitator (whose driving taught us more about how to pray!) to meet the sibling group of four. We walked into the chief inspector's office, where we discovered that the kids' files had already been pulled aside because they were about to be placed in separate foster homes the following week. By God's gracious providence, we had arrived just in time.

> Our heads were spinning from the rapid Russian discourse, and then the four kids walked in . . . holding hands.

We then went to the orphanage where we met a vivacious orphanage director speaking Russian rapidly, asking us if we wanted tea and if there were alligators in Mississippi. She kept going on about how pleasantly surprised she was that we would consider adopting four kids. She repeatedly asked, "How old are you?" and "Are you sure about this?"

Our heads were spinning from the rapid Russian discourse, and then the four kids walked in . . . holding hands. Shoes torn, clothes looking ragged, faces pale, and they didn't know what was going on. We gave them a few gifts and tried to greet them lovingly. The girls were thrilled with a stuffed animal, and James immediately began playing with his car.

The orphanage director told them that we were interested in taking them home forever. She told them that if they were to go with us, they would get a bedroom, a bike, and other goodies, but to stay would mean they would get nothing! (She actually said that.) Then she said, "But it's your decision." She went to each child to ask her or his decision, and they each said yes. Then she had the kids leave the room and asked us for our response. When she asked us if we wanted to take the kids home, it was like asking me if I wanted red meat for dinner, "Yes, of course." So the process began.

James then wrote a letter for the court saying he wanted to be adopted along with his sisters. The words were written in Russian on plain white paper with the sentence slowly drifting downward (I wish I had that letter). We then met one of James's teachers and she was quick to tell us of all the stuff that James could do. He simply shook his head and smiled. She then told us that the kids in her class recently sang a "mama song" that contains lines about longing for a mama. This precious teacher told us that a few days earlier, James refused to sing it because he didn't believe he would ever have a mama.

Eleven days later we had a court date. We picked up the kids and prepared for the legal process. Kimberly stood up first and the kind judge asked her a series of questions like, "Are you ready to give up your quiet life?" After Kimberly finished speaking eloquently, I stood up and had to speak to the judge and present my request:

Your honor, I believe every child on earth is valuable and deserving of a loving family. We believe that we can provide a loving family for these children. The world is full of orphans. And after studying all of the possible locations, having traveled to Ukraine, and having interacted with adopted Ukrainian children, we believe that this is where we are supposed to be. And I would like to ask your kind permission to adopt these children, to change their names to James Arthur, Angela Grace, Jana Sophia, and Victoria Joy, as well as to change their birth certificates, making us the official parents of the children.

One by one, the judge addressed the kids. He asked them things like,
"Do you want to go with these people?"
"Where are you going?"
"What are their names?" (To which, James said, "Mama and Papa.")

When he got to our smallest, Victoria Joy, he asked her, "Have you ever been anywhere outside of Mattviika?"

She said, "I went to the circus one time." It was priceless. The whole court erupted into laughter.

The judge granted our petition, and after a few more weeks, we were all set to return to the United States. As we worked to complete the remaining in-country documents during our last few days, one of the workers asked us if we knew what the kids' mother's name was. We didn't. She told us and we were overwhelmed. You see, Kimberly had dreams about having a daughter named Lydia and had told her sisters, who were having babies, to reserve that name for her daughter. But since we liked the girls' first names (Angela, Victoria, and Jana), we decided not to use this name. So, when the worker told us, "The birthmother's name was Lydia," we were astonished. We actually did have a Lydia that will forever be part of our story. God continued to confirm His purposes for us through numerous experiences like this one.

I will never forget our last day there. We took each kid a backpack with some new clothes that we had bought at Mothercare. Kimberly gathered the two older kids, and I took the two younger ones. These little girls went nuts over the clothes! They began counting their socks and giggling over their new outfits. They immediately took off the clothes they had worn everyday since we had been there, put on their new denim jumpers, and took the old clothes back to the class (underwear and all!). I couldn't help but think of Paul's words about how Christians, rescued by God, have put off the old clothes, and put on the new clothes in Christ Jesus (Ephesians 4:22–24; Colossians 3:5–14). A radical change in identity had taken place.

Overall, we spent 40 days in Ukraine. Before getting on our train, our driver, who spoke little English, said, "These kids have no hope in our country." Reportedly, 70 percent of unadopted girls end up in prostitution and 80 percent of the boys end up in a life of crime. Hearing him say thank you caused me to swell up in tears. We boarded an overnight train with Happy Meals from McDonald's, a piece of the homeland. We were alone with the kids for the first time, with little means of communicating, journeying back to Kiev and eventually to Hattiesburg. James began to snore that night. It was the sweetest sound I'd ever heard.

> These kids have no hope in our country.

When our 27-hour trip was over and we got off the plane in Hattiesburg, I saw Kimberly's dad, a man I respect, who is a father of four. I was so ready to weep by this time. I put my head in his chest, and we both began to sob like prom queens! Many members of our church greeted us at the airport, and when we got home, our house was decorated (and adapted for four instead of two!) with pictures of the kids and us on the mantle and in the bedrooms. And so it began.

GOD'S ADOPTION OF US

*O*f course, the greater work of grace is not our adoption of kids, but God's adoption of us, through Jesus Christ. Traveling to another country to adopt is one thing, but for God to leave heaven for earth and adopt sinners is an act of amazing grace. It's important for us to consider the similarities between God's "vertical adoption" of sinners and our "horizontal adoption" of kids.

Apostle Paul uses the word for "adoption" (*huiothesia*, meaning, "to place as a son") only five times in the New Testament, even though the concept itself is taught elsewhere in Scripture. These five occurrences appear in Paul's letters to three churches of a decidedly Roman background: Galatia, Ephesus, and Rome (Galatians 4:5; Romans 8:15, 23; 9:4, and Ephesians 1:5). Other than the one reference where Paul spoke of the Old Testament idea of Israel's special position as God's children (Romans 9:4), the remaining four references describe how spiritual orphans become God's children.

This picture of adoption is central for understanding the gospel because it involves the full scope of God's gracious work of salvation—past, present, and future are all seen in this description of salvation as adoption. God chose us in eternity past (Ephesians 1:5), He brought us to a place of faith in the present, and He promises to complete what has started on earth in the future. Regarding our future, we understand that we are adopted "now" (Romans 8:15; Galatians 4:5) but have "not yet" received the fullness of God's grace that will be revealed to us when He returns (Romans 8:23).

Indeed, the doctrine of adoption is deep and glorious. John Piper presents "eight similarities" about God's adoption of us and our adoption of children in his sermon, "Adoption: The Heart of the Gospel." I'm indebted to Piper for first pointing out these similarities to me. I've meditated on them for a few years now, as I've considered them in view of my family's adoption story. As you read, I pray you will be freshly amazed by God's adopting mercy and grace. As a result, may this understanding of God's grace to you spill over into practical acts of mercy for the fatherless in our world.

ADOPTION INVOLVES PURPOSEFUL PLANNING

*O*ur adoption of children takes serious planning. Kimberly and I had to make arrangements. We got a minivan. We changed the rooms. We thought about names. We looked at financial matters.

A lot of work goes into this planning, and a lot of resolve to finish the work. But God's plans of spiritual adoption are far superior.

Paul writes to the Galatians:

> *But when the fullness of time had come, God sent forth his Son, born of*
> *woman, born under the law, to redeem those who were under the law,*
> *so that we might receive adoption as sons. And because you are sons,*
> *God has sent the Spirit of his Son into our hearts, crying,*
> *"Abba! Father!" So you are no longer a slave, but a son,*
> *and if a son, then an heir through God.*
>
> —Galatians 4:4–7

Notice in the first line, "*the fullness of time*". According to God's divine timetable, God sent forth Christ to redeem and adopt us for His glory. In other words, this wasn't the last resort for God. No, it was His sovereign plan. At just the right time, God sent forth the Savior on a rescue mission.

To the Ephesians, Paul reaches back before the foundation of the world and says:

> *Even as he chose us in him before the foundation of the world,*
> *that we should be holy and blameless before him. In love he*
> *predestined us for adoption as sons through Jesus Christ,*
> *according to the purpose of his will.*
>
> —Ephesians 1:4–5

Paul heaps phrase upon phrase to show us God's wise and gracious plan. He says that God purposed to adopt us "*before the foundation of the world*" and that He "*predestined us for adoption as sons.*"

I admit that I cannot fully understand this dimension of God's grace. I think it's beyond the reach of my three-pound, fallen brain to fully comprehend. What is clear to me is that Paul writes Ephesians 1 as one lengthy sentence of worship (note the phrases, "*blessed*" [1:3] "*to the praise of his glorious grace*" [1:6]; "*to the praise of his glory*" [1:12]; "*to the praise of his glory*" [1:14]). Paul clearly intends for his readers to be swept up in the worship of the Triune God who has lavished grace upon sinners. It's sad when people prefer to read this passage and only play philosophical gymnastics, trying to explain how human choice and God's sovereignty work together. Both are taught in Scripture. Don't miss the point: If you know Christ, you should fall on your face in worship before the Father because it's only by His gracious plan that you do.

ADOPTION REQUIRES THE RIGHT QUALIFICATIONS

Not everyone is allowed to adopt children. This is a good thing. The world is full of crazy people who wish to harm children. Consequently, those who wish to adopt children must go through a series of background checks and questioning sessions. Our social workers and governmental workers knew more about me by the time we were finished than my parents know! They checked our finances. They checked to see if our home was suitable and safe for children. They checked our past history. We had to meet certain qualifications.

Jesus Christ alone had all the right qualifications to save us and make us children of God. Paul says, *"God sent forth his Son, born of woman"* (Galatians 4:4). Notice that God *"sent . . . his Son"* but He was *"born of woman."* Which was it? Both. This verse causes us to consider the virgin birth and the incarnation. Only Jesus was qualified to redeem and adopt us because only He is the God-man. Only Christ could be the mediator between man and God (1 Timothy 2:5); only Christ could be our sympathetic high priest (Hebrews 4:15); only Christ could be the Savior because He is the only one with all the credentials. His blood on the Cross was the blood of God (Acts 20:28), atoning for the sins of finite creatures, making us ex-orphans. Praise God, the Son, the only One who could rescue us, did just that!

> Jesus Christ alone had all the right qualifications to save us and make us children of God.

ADOPTION IS COSTLY

Perhaps the biggest question and obstacle to adoption is the price. It costs a lot of money to adopt children. It also costs time, commitment, and painful changes. It's not the path of least resistance. Kimberly and I had to go through physicals, background checks, and a number of interviews and questioning segments, along with the worries about how to pay for it all. We were told adopting one child would be about $16,000, plus travel and paperwork.

Galatians 4 reminds us that it cost God the Father infinitely more to adopt us. Paul writes, *"God sent forth his Son, born of woman, born under the law, to redeem those who were under the law,* so that we might receive adoption as sons" (1 Timothy 2:5; emphasis added). Jesus redeemed us. He purchased us. He freed us. How? Paul answers that in Galatians 3:

> *Christ redeemed us from the curse of the law by becoming a curse for us—for it is written, "Cursed is everyone who is hanged on a tree."*
> —Galatians 3:13

While it costs us a lot to adopt children, it cost God the blood of His own Son. It cost Christ to give up His whole life, in obedience to the Father. Christ, the one who *"endured the cross"* (Hebrews 12:1–2) came to redeem us and make us part of the family.

ADOPTION SAVES CHILDREN FROM TERRIBLE SITUATIONS

*A*ny kid without a mom or dad is in a terrible situation. That alone is devastating enough. Others have added to this terrible emotional and physical abuse from their past. Some are sick. Others are depressed and hopeless. Before the orphanage picked up my sister's son, Beniam, he was living on the streets, and just three years old. Her next addition to the family, a little girl they named Mercy, was diagnosed with HIV.

Millions of other orphans have never experienced some of the enjoyments that we take for granted. No Christmas. No birthdays. No dad to take them to a baseball game; no mom to help them do multiplication; no one to tuck them in at night and pray with them. No family vacations. No father-daughter dates. No father-son fishing trips. Perhaps my most vivid memory of the state of orphans in orphanages was seeing about 25 beds in one room. There was barely room to go through there. I think about that picture when I hear Steven Curtis Chapman's song "Heaven Is a Place" when he says, *"When there's no one left in the orphan's bed."* I long for the new heaven and new earth, when orphanages are no longer necessary.

Without minimizing the terrible experiences of orphans, I want to remind you that we were in a worse state spiritually. Paul tells the Ephesians that we were dead in our sins; that we followed Satan; that we were full of disobedience and depravity; and objects of God's wrath (Ephesians 2:1–3). And then he uses those two words that are so sweet, *"But God."* He said, *"But God . . . made us alive together with Christ"* (Ephesians 2:4–5). Out of God's grace and mercy, He brought us out of our terrible situations and brought us into a relationship with Him through the blood of Christ (Ephesians 2:13). In Galatians, he says that God took us from slavery to sonship (Galatians 4:1–7). Don't ever get over the fact that when we were hopeless, without God and under the judgment of God, God came in His mercy to make us part of the family in Christ Jesus.

ADOPTION INVOLVES A LEGAL CHANGE

*W*hen we set out to adopt, and then selected our kids, it was not official until the legal process was over. I will never forget when the judge slammed the gavel and made the children legally ours. Everything at that point changed. They were our children. Their birth certificates would state that we were the parents, and they bore our name. The identities of the children changed forever. Even though they were outside our families, they were legally declared our children by the one with the authority to declare it so.

Theologically, Christians share a greater blessing. Salvation is often described with terms like *justification* (declared righteous), *redemption* (set free), or *reconciliation* (at peace with God). The concept of justification is taken from the courtroom. God declares us righteous before Himself based upon the work of Christ, who took the penalty that we deserved. By faith in Christ, God credits to us the merits of Jesus.

> I will never forget when the judge slammed the gavel and made the children legally ours.

But our salvation is not just a legal transfer. It begins with a transfer, but it leads to a familial relationship. Our spiritual identity has changed. We are legally God's children. This is why J. I. Packer says, "Adoption is the highest privilege of the Gospel; higher even than justification." It's not more important than justification. You must be right with

God the Judge. But it doesn't stop there. This legal transfer brings you into the family of God.

ADOPTION INVOLVES THE SPIRIT OF SONSHIP

I wondered how the children would respond to us, and how long it would take for them to call us Mom and Dad. I'll never forget the second day in the orphanage when Angela said, "Mama" and the next day when she said, "Papa." I know these are our kids, not just because the legal work is done, but because of experiential connection we share. That's why when people ask us how our lives have changed I tell them that it just seems natural. There is a mysterious element in adopting children that's hard to express.

Similarly, Paul reminds the Galatians that God *"sent the Spirit of his son into our hearts, crying "Abba! Father."* *Abba* was a term of endearment. It was a word Jesus used when He was praying in Gethsemane, *"Abba Father"* (Mark 14:36). Everywhere Christians go they can be sure that their Abba Father is with them because of the Spirit of sonship in our hearts. To the Romans, Paul writes, *"You have received a spirit of adoption as sons, by whom we cry 'Abba! Father!' The Spirit Himself bears witness with our spirit that we are children of God"* (Romans 8:15–16). Because we have the Spirit of sonship we need to not fear, but trust and obey in our heavenly Father.

ADOPTION TRANSFORMS THE CHILD IN EVERY WAY

I remember visiting my sister during the early days of their adoption. Derara was watching television. I asked him what he was watching, and he said, *Walker, Texas Ranger.* It was his favorite show. Beniam could show me how different baseball players stood at home plate preparing to hit (even though he had never seen a baseball game in Ethiopia). The boys took on phrases, mannerisms, and the language of their parents. They bore all the marks of the family.

I'll never forget an example of James taking after his father. My first Sunday back home, I was leaving around 3:00 P.M. to return to the church for the 6:00 P.M. service. James insisted on going with me, even though he had many new toys to enjoy. I told him it would be a while, but he said, "Me, church." He sat with me in the study as I prepared and then went with me to sit in the front row. I looked over at him and saw that he had his *Jesus Story Book Bible*, his water bottle, and his toy cell phone. I was also carrying a Bible, a cell phone, and a water bottle!

When we are adopted spiritually, everything begins to change because God begins sanctifying us, making us like His Son. Paul says, *"All who are led by the Spirit of God are sons of God"* (Romans 8:14). We begin to walk according to the will of the Father, bear the marks of the Father, and imitate the Father (Ephesians 5:1). In fact, Jesus says true followers of His desire to let others see our good deeds and give glory to our Father who is in heaven (Matthew 5:16). That is a radically different pursuit than a world who doesn't know Christ (but desperately needs to know Him!).

ADOPTION GIVES THE CHILD THE RIGHT TO BE AN HEIR OF THE FATHER

*I*f God in His gracious providence gives Kimberly and me biological children, then we would include them in our will the same way that our adopted children will be included. Our four kids are our heirs. They will never be treated less than children that we may have biologically. They will inherit whatever we have.

Spiritually, we are heirs of God. Paul says, *"If children, then heirs—heirs of God and fellow heirs with Christ"* (Romans 8:17). To the Galatians he says, *"If a son, then an heir through God"* (Galatians 4:7). Paul draws on the Roman background to make these theological statements. Interestingly, several Roman emperors adopted boys for the purpose of conferring on them certain authorities and privileges. Julius Caesar adopted Octavian; Octavian adopted

> "Whom have I in heaven but you [O LORD]? And there is nothing on earth that I desire, besides you."

Tiberius, who adopted Gaius Caligula. Gaius Caligula's uncle adopted Nero just four years before Paul wrote Romans. He and the other rulers were legally sons. We have been given something infinitely greater; namely, the privileges and blessings that come from being an heir of the Father of glory!

The value of the inheritance is determined by the worth of the one who gives it. Our glorious God promises to grant us an inheritance; and in fact, He Himself is our inheritance! Of all the things God could give us, the most precious satisfying reward in the universe is God Himself. The psalmist said, *"Whom have I in heaven but you [O LORD]? And there is nothing on earth that I desire besides you"* (Psalm 73:25). God's people will dwell in God's presence forever, and there will be nothing more satisfying than this (Revelation 21:3).

Because of the glory of our inheritance that awaits us, we struggle on earth. Paul says that this present suffering produces holy longings for our "future adoption." He says, *"[We] who have the firstfruits of the Spirit, groan inwardly as we wait eagerly for adoption as sons, the redemption of our bodies"* (Romans 8:23). In light of the unspeakable joy that awaits the believer when his adoption is fully realized, Paul could write these encouraging words:

> *For I consider that the sufferings of this present time are not worth comparing with the glory that is to be revealed to us.*
>
> —Romans 8:18

Be encouraged, child of God. Your inheritance awaits you. You will be with your Father forever, apart from the presence of sin, in the warmth of His eternal presence.

GOD SAVES

As I write this paragraph, Kimberly and I are weeks away from traveling to Ethiopia to adopt our fifth child, a son from Ethiopia. We desired a brother for James and wanted to adopt from another part of the world. When prospective boys were shown to us, our hearts leaped for a little boy named Eyasu, which is basically Joshua in English. Joshua's biological parents died of an illness, and he has no siblings. Interestingly, the name Joshua means "The Lord saves." What a perfect name! It will serve forever to remind us (and him) that our adoption of Joshua is only a reflection of the most important adoption, the spiritual one that comes from the God who saves spiritual orphans.

Indeed, the gospel transforms not only our identity and eternal destiny, but when rightly understood and applied, it will also transform how we see the world and serve the world. Let us meditate much on the doctrine of God's adoption of us. The name might not be Joshua, but it might as well be, if we are Christian. God saved us from our desperate condition, through Jesus (whose name in the Greek Old Testament is exactly the same as "Joshua"). May we continue to grow in our gratitude to the God who saves, and may we radically extend His redeeming love to a world in need.

See the need of the orphan. Feel the need and consider doing something of eternal value by caring for the fatherless in practical ways. Consider adoption. Help adoptive parents. Raise awareness. Develop a fund. Host orphans. Underwrite an orphanage. Do something. Do something for the good of the fatherless and the glory of the God who has made us ex-orphans through Jesus Christ.

— TM

CONTEMPLATING HOW ADOPTION SHOWS THE GOSPEL AND CARES FOR ORPHANS AS GOD INTENDS

AN ORPHAN STORY— RYAN AND LISA BOND

A little over four years ago I sat in a Wednesday night service at Southland Christian Church and watched a film about the fallout of the HIV/AIDS crisis. Orphans. Millions. My seven-year-old son, Noah, sat to the left of me, and my husband of two years sat to his left. I watched as my young son's face resonated with the children on the screen. His father is Ethiopian. He looked up at me with big, tear-filled eyes and said, "Momma, they're Ethiopian like me!" As tears streamed down my face, I thought, *But they are not like you. They have no parents to love them.* I then felt God's voice stronger than I had ever felt: *Some of those will be your children.* I sat in stunned silence for a few minutes. *My children? Really God? Did you forget about my past?* You see, I had been forgiven much. The natural response to that type of forgiveness is to love much (see Luke 7:47).

> "Well He's not calling me. We have our hands full already. Three is enough."

I kept this quiet for a couple of months (not my norm). On a long drive with my husband I said, "God is calling me to adopt some kids from Ethiopia."

He grunted and said, "Well He's not calling me. We have our hands full already. Three is enough." Ryan, married previous to our marriage, had two children, Adam and Lauren, who came to us on school breaks and for the summer. You know what I said back? Nothing! Now that's the work of the Holy Spirit. I just sat quietly knowing.

Many months passed with little talk about adoption. Then on the morning of May 9, my and Ryan's birthday, I woke up to a letter on my nightstand. A letter and a check! The letter read, "I am ready. I feel it too." The check was enough for the home study.

Two months later, I was cooking dinner and received a call from our case manager. She asked if I had looked at the waiting child photo listing.

"Yes."

She asked if I was interested in anyone in particular.

"I don't know."

She knew of our desire to adopt two boys and my preference that they would not be leaving behind other siblings. She sent me to my computer screen to look at two unrelated boys. I had looked at them earlier because I was looking for siblings. She told me the older of the two, Derara, seven, was leaving behind a little sister who was dying.

"It would help him if you adopted another younger child at the same time," she said. She then led me to a three- or four-year-old boy named Beniam, who had been living on the streets. He had great big eyes and no smile.

And I knew. I slid in my computer chair, put my face in my hands, and wept. After gaining some composure I called my husband. Still crying, I whispered, "I just saw our boys!"

Six months later, Ryan, Noah, Noah's dad (Dawit), and I boarded Ethiopian Airlines to go pick up our young sons. We arrived in Addis Ababa on December 31. We were met at the airport by Dawit's cousin, who drove us to his parents' house where we spent our first night. After greeting Noah's aunt and uncle and having a meal, we turned in for the night. None of us slept, not a wink. Ryan, Noah, and I shared a room with twin beds, and we simply lay there talking. Like kids on Christmas eve, the morning couldn't come quickly enough.

The day you meet your adopted children is like no other day in your life. We were driven into the compound and my mind was a swirl of questioning thoughts: *What if I don't recognize them? What if they don't like me? What if I don't know what to say?* As we pulled through the gates of the compound,

I saw him . . . Derara. He was wearing his traditional Ethiopian clothes. I began to cry, knowing that this child—this special gift—had put on his best for us. This, the day he got new parents, he wanted to look his best.

We got out of the cab; he came over to us; and I wrapped him in my arms. I loved him. I loved him before I ever knew him. Before he was ever born, God knew this moment would take place. As he left my arms and went to Ryan's, little Beniam Teraku inched toward me. I picked him up and held him. He was so tiny. He looked so sad. I prayed for strength to help him heal from the hurts he'd experienced already in his young life. Dawit was behind us snapping pictures. He wasn't there for the birth of our son Noah, but he was our cameraman for the birth of our new family. Derara and Beniam were not the only ones getting a front-row seat to God's redemptive, restorative character.

A few months after we had been home, Noah came downstairs and said, "Momma, Derara is crying for his little sister. He does this every night."

I went upstairs, climbed in bed behind him, curled up, and cried with him. "We will find her. We will find her, and we will bring her home," I whispered.

The next morning, I emailed our pastor and relayed the story Derara had shared with us of his sister being taken from him during the night at his first orphanage. I told him we wanted to find her, and we wanted to bring her home. Somehow I knew she wasn't dead. He invited us onstage to be prayed over that same weekend. We were onstage on a Saturday night. Kaleab was found Tuesday! One orphan girl among millions! We started our paperwork.

> We wanted to find her and we wanted to bring her home. Somehow I knew she wasn't dead.

One year later, as we began preparations to go pick up Kaleab, we were again summoned to Derara's bedside. By this time, he was speaking English and had told us about his whole family and the deaths of his parents. "I want you to find my older brothers and sister and give them the money I have in my bank account." He had about two hundred dollars in his account. We contacted the attorney who had worked with us on his adoption. He said he knew where the family lived and could take us there when we arrived. Less than two years from our first adoption, we boarded the flight to pick up our baby girl, four-year-old Kaleab.

We met her the day after our arrival in Ethiopia. The drive was filled with much the same emotion as on our first trip. When the gate to the compound opened, my heart leaped. I was scanning the porch for her; it was full with about ten little snotty-nosed four-year-olds, and I didn't see her—and then she came out slowly on the hand of the nanny, walking down the stairs, both shy and proud, and I began to cry. She was—she is—so beautiful.

The next day found us in a car to Woliso, Ethiopia; we were going to meet Kaleab and Derara's older brother and sister. I was dreaming of which of those four-year-olds I'd come back for the next year when I again sensed God speak to me. I knew this drive was not to visit my children's siblings but to visit my children! I wrestled with God. *God I don't want these old kids. It's too hard. God I want one of the little ones. Isn't that enough? I can't do this.* I kept hearing in my heart: *"I know the plans I have for you, plans to prosper and not to harm you. Plans to give you a hope and a future"* (Jeremiah 29:11).

We met Selamawit, Biruk, and Guta at the gate of their home, a small three-roomed shanty. Selam and Guta were thrilled to see Kaleab, showering her with kisses, and they were gracious and friendly with us. Biruk was guarded and standoffish.

We spent the afternoon showing them pictures of Derara and other family. They shared a meal with us. We got to meet aunts, uncles, cousins, and even Grandma. That evening, we left, heavy-hearted, knowing we were leaving our family behind. Knowing, as Biruk had told us, he was sending Selam and Guta to Immanuel orphanage. He could no longer afford to feed them.

Shortly after we arrived back in the US, we began making the necessary contacts to adopt these two older siblings. Funny how less than three years ago, I wanted no girls. I wanted a child who was leaving behind no other siblings, and now we were planning our fourth and fifth adoptions. What I had thought of as harmful to me, God meant for good (Genesis 50:20).

One year later, we boarded a plane to Ethiopia. This time, we were accompanied by ten-year-old Derara. His grandma didn't even know it, but she was getting her wish to see her grandbaby once again.

We arrived in Ethiopia, and our case manager told us that she had a surprise for us. We walked up the stairs of the guesthouse to our room, and out of the door bounded Selam and Guta! We all hugged and cried. And we all thanked God for His goodness and His faithfulness!

In six years, we went from one child to eight! There have been hard times. There has been opposition. I had to change and learn how to be this "megamom."

I still have work to do. People often ask me how I do it: "How do you keep up with the laundry? How do you get everyone to their activities? How do you spend time with each child?" The answer is simple: *I* don't.

— RBL

We must recognize that God has placed in us the call to go to the orphan to ease his and her suffering.

2

WHAT IS THE STATE OF THE FATHERLESS WORLDWIDE?

*I*n the following chapters, we will further establish that God intends for His people to care for orphans—as He has cared for us—and see that the church has a long history of active engagement in addressing the needs of orphans. The question that faces us as present-day followers of Jesus is, *How do we, in our context, live out God's heart and continue the church's history for orphan care?* This is a huge question with huge implications for us and for our churches.

The temptation is to be so overwhelmed by the need that we fail to take time to perceive the situation accurately as our foundation for how we choose to minister to fatherless children. Think about it like this. Would you set out on a big construction project without surveying the site and trying to understand the site that you are about to build upon? If you chose not to take time to assess, everything with your building project might turn out just fine, but more likely, a failure to understand the "lay of the land" will result in a lot of meaningless work, wasted resources, burdensome delays, and unnecessary frustration.

Frankly, the world's orphan problem is too vast for us to be wasteful of the precious resources that God gives us to meet it. So, let's wade in slowly and consider the needs before we begin to think about our response. Then we can really be prepared to address the question of where God would have us spend our efforts in ministering through today's global orphan situation.

How many orphans are currently living on the earth? It seems like a pretty straightforward question, and you may be surprised by the difficulty in answering it. According to the United Nations Children's Fund (UNICEF), there are estimated to be between 143 and 210 million orphans worldwide, though this number uncertain. While this estimate is staggering, it likely fails to give a full picture of the scope of the problem. You see, UNICEF only includes children who have lost one or both parents to death in its calculation of the worldwide orphan population. While this approach to defining who is an orphan isn't really wrong, it does fail to account for many of the children that are truly fatherless.

To begin, UNICEF does not take into account the numerous orphaned children whose living parents have abandoned them to institutions or life on the street. These children are no less orphans in a practical sense than those who have experienced the death of a parent. In fact, in many cases those children who have been abandoned may be in more peril than a child who fits the technical UN definition of being orphaned.

UNICEF estimates also do not reflect sold or trafficked children who are living in slavery or orphans living in those countries (mostly Middle Eastern Islamic nations) that fail to report orphan statistics. Truly, we have no way of knowing how many children may be orphaned and unaccounted for in today's statistics. What we do know is that the numbers of fatherless children are astounding, and we know that God has given Christ followers the mission of caring for them in their hardship.

While it may be enlightening or even inspiring to look at the statistics about the world's orphan problem, the church cannot be satisfied merely to understand the problem. We must recognize that God has placed in us the call to go to the orphan to ease his and her suffering. Yes, to understand is key to building strategies to address the orphan crisis, but we cannot be satisfied just to know about orphans and their struggles or be intimidated into doing nothing because the problem seems too big. We as the church must be ever conscious that we have a responsibility to discover ways to minister to every orphan on the face of the globe. It is our responsibility.

No matter how insurmountable the problem seems, we must be active in sharing the love and compassion of Christ with orphans as a means of showing and spreading His gospel. Day-to-day, I think it helps to focus more on the small picture than the big. How are we working today to make a difference on Jesus' behalf in the life of an orphan?

So, in looking for ways to break down the enormous challenge that the huge mass of orphans in the world presents, it is helpful to consider some overarching facts. As we analyze these facts and statistics, some common trends and patterns of need emerge, and those patterns can be helpful in targeting our prayer and our work. As we look to understand the crisis, we can begin to see some very practical ways for the church to respond and live out its mission to the fatherless. What follows in this chapter are some observations that have guided our thinking about ministering to orphans, along with more stories that reinforce our hope that not only are we called, but we can respond.

ORPHAN MINISTRY IS NOT JUST AN ISSUE FOR THE REST OF THE WORLD. There is an orphan crisis in America. It may be easy for us to believe that America has conquered the orphan problem. After all, we have virtually eliminated orphanages. We no longer send orphaned and abandoned children westward on trains to be placed out to frontier families as we did in the 1800s. Today, we have a fully functional foster-care system that places children into homes (or institutions) that are, at least theoretically, well prepared and well suited to care for them and to launch them into adulthood. As we will discuss later, our institutional system of foster care isn't enough. Today, upwards of a half-million children are in the foster-care system in America, and approximately 130 thousand of

> A half-million children are in the foster-care system in America. 130,000 of those children are immediately adoptable.

those children are immediately adoptable. With nearly 225 million professing Christian adults in America, no identifiable reason exists that all of these children cannot be placed immediately in the care of loving Christian families who can nurture them with the love of Christ as they grow to adulthood.

ORPHAN MINISTRY IS NOT SIMPLY AN ADOPTION ISSUE. Globally, the number of orphans who are actually eligible for adoption is at best a small fractional percentage of the total number. Many reasons exist for this fact. In some cases, institutionalized children are not complete orphans. For instance, of the 750,000 Russian children living in institutions or in alternative family care, approximately 17 percent are actually without both parents. The long-term hope for many of these incomplete orphans and their parents (or guardians) is for a reunification of their families at some point in the future. In some cases, the children are institutionalized as a result of economic or health-related hardship, but parental rights to these children remain as the families are assumed by the system to be striving toward bringing their children home. Also, many orphaned children live in countries in which inter-country adoption is not permitted, and where the social and economic climate makes the possibility of their adoption remote at best. While we may believe that adoption is a practice that is both theologically desirable in its display of the gospel and practically beneficial as it brings children into a family for love and support, we must concede that adoption is not the only answer for the church as it ignores our ultimate responsibility to care for all orphans.

ORPHAN MINISTRY MEANS ACTIVELY PROMOTING AND SUPPORTING ADOPTION. The church—the body of Christ—needs to actively uphold adoption as a viable means of mercy ministry. We have already discussed the theological aspects of adoption. To live out adoption as a God-based gospel initiative, churches must make adoption a part of their ministry and mission strategy. Adoption is a difficult and often expensive process. A churchwide emphasis on adoption is necessary if individual Christians in significant numbers are going to embrace the mandate to care for orphans through adoption. A portion of the pastoral role in leading the church to minister for orphans is casting a vision for orphan care that is accessible to everyone. Individual Christians, no matter our age or life circumstance, also need to see how God can use us in caring for the fatherless. An intentional church strategy must involve practical plans and actions that everyone can take to minister.

As part of a plan for discipleship, churches can offer great support before the adoption process by helping families to know about and pursue the available adoption options. As communities, churches can help families to afford adoptions by sharing the expense across the body. As families move through the often-turbulent adoption process, the church can provide programs intended to support and encourage families along the way. Finally, the church can be a great community of resources to hold families up through the challenges that lie ahead as they adjust to the new reality of being adoptive families.

Another role for the church is to expand the frame of reference that church members have for adoption. Adoption is not only about babies. Churches must sound the call that literally millions of older children are waiting to be adopted into families, and our adoption in Christ compels us to adopt them as well.

ORPHAN MINISTRY MEANS BEING ENGAGED IN INSTITUTIONAL ORPHAN CARE. Current estimates indicate that approximately 10 million orphans live in institutions throughout the globe. While the lives of all orphans are of concern to the church, the plight of these children is particularly bleak.

Studies reveal that children living in institutions are much more likely to experience violence and sexual abuse when compared to orphans being reared in a foster-care environment. Generally, institutionalized orphans also suffer from poorer life outcomes. Orphan graduates, those children who attain majority age while in the institution and who are subsequently released to live independently, face few options and great desperation in finding a life beyond the institution. In Ukraine, for instance, the typical orphan graduate "ages out" of the system at age 16, at least one year shy of a completed secondary education, with little potential for further education or employment. With little or no option, these young adults commonly turn to crime and prostitution as a means of survival. The desperation drives many to suicide with as many as 10 percent taking their lives before the age of 18. Life prior to their graduation gives few of these kids reason to hope for the future. Their days are spent in the relatively cold seclusion of the orphanage without experiences that show them a life beyond what they experience in the institution. Many spend their entire lives segregated from the mainstream of society. They are confined to the institution for sleeping, eating, playing, schooling, and even extracurricular activities. The church must work to minister to children in

> The desperation drives many to suicide with as many as 10 percent taking their lives before the age of 18.

institutions who are unadoptable, either by family ties or government policy.

Another issue of significance is how the church should minister to orphan graduates once they are on their own. Because they have grown up in regimented institutions that poorly reflect life "on the outside," these children are often poorly equipped to live independently. They lack the basic life skills and emotional stability to function independently. Helping orphan graduates through transitional assistance is a practical way that the church can meet their needs and can expose them to Christ and to life from a Christian worldview perspective.

ORPHAN MINISTRY MEANS BEING ENGAGED IN THE FIGHT AGAINST SLAVERY AND HUMAN TRAFFICKING. The world's orphan and human trafficking crises are inextricably linked. Obviously, orphans are among the least powerful and most vulnerable people on earth. That is why I believe that God has been so direct in His call to care for them. They are defenseless, and God by His very nature is a defender. In His call to emulate His holiness, He wants us to be defenders as well. From their lack of standing and significance in society, orphaned children are easy to exploit. Mostly, when they are taken, they are not missed. When they are abused, they are not heard. And sadly, there is a seemingly endless supply of orphans to be used and cast aside by a depraved system of abusers.

According to the US State Department, somewhere between 600,000 and 800,000 people are trafficked across international borders each year, and approximately 50 percent of those trafficked are children. Orphan children can find themselves in dire circumstances, serving in forced labor and even prostitution at the hands of a well organized and lucrative global criminal system bent on their exploitation for the gain of others. Some children are sold into slavery by their families or are given by their families on the promise of a better life for the child, and thus they are rendered fatherless in the process. Others are abducted into slavery from the streets with no one to notice their absence or to come looking for them. Still others are among the orphan graduates described above. These "graduates" are targets of desperation for human traders and pimps. With nowhere to turn for the basic necessities of life, they give up the one commodity they possess—themselves—to pay the price for their subsistence.

As ambassadors of Christ, we must stand in the gap for these helpless children. They are our concern because they are God's handiwork, and they are being treated unjustly. The presence of this kind of injustice is dishonoring to God. To God's glory from His example, we must look for practical ways to care for exploited orphans and to rescue them from their oppressors. How can we as individuals and as churches take part in making a difference for a vulnerable orphan? We have to be creative to make a real difference. While we must look for little, personal ways to rescue exploited orphans, we also need to band together and use the collective voice of the church. We must stand up as citizens and voters to insist that our local, state, and national governments take action on orphans' behalf. We must use our place in the world as a tool of pressure to make laws that fight back the slavery and oppression of these precious children.

ORPHAN CARE MEANS BEING ENGAGED IN TRANSRACIAL MINISTRY. A further complication to the world's orphan situation is the global AIDS crisis. Much of the coming wave of new orphans in the world will be from Africa, the most AIDS-affected continent. According to the July 2004 UNICEF Report on AIDS, "Sub-Saharan Africa is home to 24 of the 25 countries with the world's highest levels of HIV prevalence, and the fastest growing proportions and absolute numbers of orphaned children. Between 1990 and 2003, the number of children orphaned by AIDS increased from less than one million to an estimated 12.6 million." The report goes on to state, "The impact of HIV/AIDS on mortality and the number of children orphaned by AIDS in sub-Saharan Africa will continue to increase through 2010. By then, more than one in five children will be orphaned in Botswana, Lesotho, Swaziland, and Zimbabwe." Over 14 million children have been orphaned as a result of AIDS, and the number will likely continue to grow exponentially for the foreseeable future. To compound the issue, many of these orphaned children are themselves infected with HIV. To address this issue, the church will have to cross some difficult social barriers to be sure, but they are barriers that should not exist. The sheer scope of the problem dictates that the evangelical church in America must deal with any bend toward the sin of racism if we are to meet this ministry challenge. We cannot afford to take a segregationist view of this issue. Practically and pointedly, there are likely not enough families of African heritage able to take all these children who can be adopted.

Transracial adoptions must be an option to bring those who are adoptable into loving Christian families. More pointedly, this crisis affords the church a tangible opportunity to live out a God-based ethic of racial relationships and to engage in racial reconciliation to its utmost.

The task is huge and daunting. There are no easy answers to the world's orphan crisis. We must not be paralyzed by the size of the challenge. We must focus on the power of God, as He is our challenge giver. He, not the sad state of human failing, has given us this challenge, and He will supply our needs. Just as we recognize that our adoption in Christ is not plan B in God's working out of His plan for redemption, we must take comfort that God's plan for caring for the fatherless is not just His way of dealing with a social problem. It is the gospel on display in our lives. Living out James 1:27 in our present context calls upon the body of Christ to discover a multifaceted approach to visiting and caring for the orphan. In the upcoming chapters, we will discuss some very realistic ways that churches and their members can face these issues and minister effectively in them. In fact, scattered throughout the upcoming chapters are the stories of people just like you and me who have made themselves available for God's use in various ways to love and care for orphans. Their stories are encouraging and inspiring, but most of all, they are evidence—answers—of a sovereign God who loves orphans and gives power and grace to His people to act out that love. We hope that as you continue to read, you will find hope, inspiration, a place to start, or a place to continue ministering the gospel through caring for orphans.

— RM

When it comes to caring for
the people on God's heart,
indifference is a sin.

—Tom Davis, *Fields of the Fatherless*

3

"WHY ARE YOU PUSHING ADOPTION AND ORPHAN CARE?"

*A*fter emphasizing the need for orphan care, I still get questions about why we are calling for a radical reorientation of our lives for the sake of the fatherless. The question sometimes arises from individuals who actually grew up in the church but rarely if ever heard about the subject. If they had heard, it may have been only in the form of a prayer request for someone who was considering adoption because the hopeful parents were unable to have biological children. Typical questions to potentially adoptive parents are, "Can't you have kids?" or "Don't you want your *own* kids?"

Whether or not you can have biological children really has nothing to do with the Christian's call to do orphan care. Further, we don't see adoption merely as plan B and only for parents who can't have biological children. Rather, we see both orphan care and adoption as expressions of practical Christianity.

Not only are some Christians often puzzled, unsure, or even turned off by the idea of adoption, others tend to think of orphan ministry as "the social gospel," that is, the abandoning of evangelism in order to do social ministries for those in need. Few have seen churches preach the exclusive claims of Christ boldly *and* care for the orphan and the poor mercifully. We believe Jesus did both (evangelism and mercy) and so should we. The proclamation of good news and the practice of good deeds go together.

Another reason people ask the question, "Why are you pushing for adoption and orphan care?"—much of the evangelical church has not focused on caring for the orphan as a major ministry of the church in recent years. When members in these churches hear of orphan care, a common reaction is to think that the pastor is leading a radical new movement, instead of returning to a biblical picture of a New Testament church.

Further, we think the emphasis from conservative evangelicals regarding anti-abortion protests might have actually pushed orphan ministry and adoption to the side. Many champion life—and rightly so—but fail to act on behalf of the millions of children existing with no mama or papa. My question for the anti-abortion protestors is: *Would you be willing to adopt these kids if they were not aborted?* It's one thing to declare to those you disagree with, but it's another to care for the little ones personally.

> Adoption and orphan care aren't new ideas; they're biblical ideas.

The simple and obvious fact for the Christian is this: adoption and orphan care aren't new ideas; *they're biblical ideas.* The reason we must stress them is the same reason we stress evangelism, prayer, stewardship, and other practices Scripture teaches us. Caring for all of the fatherless is enforced in God's Word, flows from God's heart, and such care embodies convictions that have marked God's people for centuries.

GETTING BACK TO BIBLICAL CONVICTIONS

There are at least four biblical convictions that should drive us to display radical love for the fatherless:

1. God is concerned for all people made in His image;
2. He has a special concern for the fatherless;
3. God commands His people to share His concern for the fatherless; and
4. He is pro-adoption.

CONVICTION 1:
GOD IS CONCERNED FOR ALL PEOPLE MADE IN HIS IMAGE.

My wife decided that the first verse we should teach our four kids was Genesis 1:1. It's a good place to start. Not only is it the first verse of the Bible, but it's also the starting point for understanding the world. God is the one and only maker of heaven and earth, who created all things by the word of His power, and continues to sustain all things and guide them to their appointed end. The Triune God is the glorious creator of all individuals. In Genesis 1, we read:

> *Then God said, "Let us make man in our image, after our likeness." ...*
> *So God created man in his own image, in the image of God he*
> *created him; male and female he created them.*
> —Genesis 1:26–27

The Triune God created mankind *intimately*, from the ground and the man's side (Genesis 2:7, 21–23); *distinctly*, as male and female (Genesis 1:27); and *purposefully*, for His glory (Isaiah 43:7; 1 Corinthians 10:31). Since people are made in the image and likeness of God, they possess dignity, value, and worth. Mankind is the pinnacle of God's creation, God's treasured possession.

Therefore, we must value what God values, and love what He loves. From the womb to the tomb, the doctrine of the image of God, *imago dei*, should affect how we view human beings. Many false ideas about humanity are popular but they must be rejected. People aren't *machines* who merely produce; we aren't simply beings *equal to animals*; we aren't *flesh alone*; we aren't just *sexual beings*; we aren't *pawns of the universe*, nor are we *gods of the universe*. People are individuals, with the capacity to think, feel, reason, love, rejoice, reproduce, choose, and most of all to know God personally and eternally through Jesus Christ (John 17:3).

After the creation of our parents in the Garden of Eden, sin entered the world and left us in a fallen place with its devastating results, including a world of orphans. Now people are affected by sin morally (we are rebellious); physically (we get sick and die); mentally, (sin affects our minds); and relationally (we are separated from God and one another). Our great need then is for spiritual regeneration, being made into new creations in Christ Jesus (2 Corinthians 5:17). The culmination of history includes Christians seeing Christ face-to-face and being changed into His likeness (1 John 3:2), forever experiencing His glory (Revelation 21–22).

Because of people's particular value as image bearers, the Christian's response should always be compassion for people. For instance, James says that we should guard our lips so that we don't "*curse people made in the likeness of God*" (James 3:9). We also reject prejudice and partiality because "*God shows no partiality*" toward those of various ethnicities (Acts 10:34). Each people group bears God's image.

Biblical examples of dishonoring children as image bearers include Herod's killing of babies during Jesus' day (following the similar evil practice of Pharaoh's killing of babies, years earlier in Egypt). Children were not held in high esteem in Roman days, as is the case in our day. By Jesus' time, it's reported that the Romans had a trash heap beside the home, where they often left unwanted children. Children were left in the dung pile or in the trash, and if people wanted the kids, they would simply pick them up. Sometimes, those who took them, raised these children to be prostitutes, gladiators, or slaves. Infant mortality was high and many died before or at a young age. In contrast, the early Christians were known for caring for abandoned children, valuing their lives.

The Christian view of children must be countercultural, reflecting Jesus' view of kids. What was Jesus' view of kids? Consider a few statements the Savior made:

> *Then children were brought to him that he might lay his hands on*
> *them and pray. The disciples rebuked the people, but Jesus said,*
> *"Let the little children come to me and do not hinder them,*
> *for to such belongs the kingdom of heaven."*
> *And he laid his hands on them and went away.*
> —Matthew 19:13–15

> *Whoever receives one such child in my name receives me, but*
> *whoever causes one of these little ones who believe in me to sin, it*
> *would be better for him to have a great millstone fastened around his*
> *neck and to be drowned in the depth of the sea.*
> —Matthew 18:15–6

And he took a child and put him in the midst of them, and taking him in
his arms, he said to them, "Whoever receives one such child in
my name receives me, and whoever receives me,
receives not me but him who sent me."

—Mark 9:36–37

In these passages, we see the Savior loving children, praying for children, and standing up for and taking up children in His arms. He even stated that to receive them, was to receive Him! Jesus displayed the biblical ethic regarding kids. We must value unborn children (Psalm 139:16); biological children (Genesis 1:28, 48:9; 1 Samuel 1:20); and orphans (Proverbs 23:10; Psalm 68:5).

In addition, the doctrine of the image of God affects how we view the poor—which includes orphans. Consider the relationship between our care for the poor and the image of God in Proverbs:

The rich and the poor meet together; the Lord is the maker of them all.

—Proverbs 22:2

The poor man and the oppressor meet together;
the Lord gives light to the eyes of both.

—Proverbs 29:13

"Whoever mocks the poor insults his Maker; he who is glad at
calamity will not go unpunished."

—Proverbs 17:5

It is no wonder that the command to care for the poor is all over the pages of our Bibles. To dishonor or deny the poor is to dishonor or deny the God who made them.

Where did you learn about the image of God? Who told you about Creator God? You probably learned it from a parent, a pastor, or a faithful Christian witness. Remember, millions of orphans have little to no knowledge of God, the *imago dei*, or of the love of Jesus. Sadly, in an orphanage, children often feel worthless, hopeless, and unlovable.

Tom Davis records in *Fields of the Fatherless* the following personal confession of a Russian orphan:

I hated my life since the third grade when I was unmercifully beaten. I felt then that life is lost and death is looking for me. And my tears were telling me that life was nothing in comparison with death. I felt like a little cockroach, which [responds in] fear when seen. A bunch of American people came to our school. I thought those people wanted to laugh at us. But I was mistaken. They are people willing to give up the most precious gift a person can possess, love. [Their] intentions to share seemed strange as they had their own kids. But these people have such big hearts to give that there is still enough room even for us little cockroaches. Then I began to feel myself not a cockroach anymore that deserved to be killed, but a little human being. It is a wonderful feeling. Believe me.

Hear the cry of the orphans who need to know that they have dignity, value, and worth as God's image bearers.

CONVICTION 2:
GOD HAS A SPECIAL CONCERN FOR THE FATHERLESS.

When you search the Scriptures, you find people are objects of God's great mercy. However, three groups of people stand out: *the orphan, the widow, and the sojourner.* Consider what God speaks about His concern for these three groups of people:

God established laws to protect and provide for them:

He [God] executes justice for the fatherless and the widow, and loves the sojourner, giving him food and clothing.
—Deuteronomy 10:18

God promises to bless those who bless them:

"At the end of every three years you shall bring out all the tithe of your produce in the same year and lay it up within your towns. And the Levite, because he has no portion or inheritance with you, and the sojourner, the fatherless, and the widow, who are within your

towns, shall come and eat and be filled, that the Lord your God may
bless you in all the work of your hands that you do."

—Deuteronomy 14:28–29

God warns those who abuse them:

"Cursed be anyone who perverts the justice due to the sojourner,
the fatherless, and the widow."

—Deuteronomy 27:19

"You shall not wrong a sojourner or oppress him, for you were
sojourners in the land of Egypt. You shall not mistreat
any widow or fatherless child."

—Exodus 22:21–22

"Do not oppress the widow, the fatherless, the sojourner, or the poor,
and let none of you devise evil against another in your heart."

—Zechariah 7:10

God promises to protect the fatherless and those w ho are lonely and helpless:

But you do see, for you note mischief and vexation, that you may take it
into your hands; to you the helpless commits himself;
you have been the helper of the fatherless.

—Psalm 10:14

The LORD is king forever and ever; the nations perish from his land.
O LORD, you hear the desire of the afflicted; you will strengthen their
heart; you will incline your ear to do justice to the fatherless and the
oppressed, so that man who is of the earth may
strike terror no more.

—Psalm 10:16–18

Father of the fatherless and protector of widows is God in his holy
habitation. God settles the solitary in a home.

—Psalm 68:5–6

The LORD watches over the sojourners; he upholds the widow and the
fatherless, but the way of the wicked he brings to ruin.

—Psalm 146:9

I've observed that many churches make noble efforts to care for widows, particularly through deacon ministry. They often keep records of how many widows are members and which deacon is assigned to each respectfully. I'm certainly in favor of this ministry. In Acts 6, the early church gave special attention to the task of caring for the widow (vv. 1–7). However, in the same churches little may have been done strategically and practically for the orphan.

Ministries of mercy should be created for the orphan and the sojourner as well as the widow. In the biblical period, these three groups were often abused. In today's world, they are often exploited and battered as well. For example, many young girls are trafficked for prostitution purposes all over the world. God expects His people to care for those who have no homes and no hope.

> Ministries of mercy should be created for the orphan and the sojourner as well as the widow.

God expected Israel to care for these groups because it reflected God's mercy toward them. Israel was the sojourner before Abraham was called to be the father of many nations. Israel was the widow until God made her His own. Israel was the orphan until God adopted them Israel as His son.

In the New Testament, God's people are called to show the same type of merciful love, to *"be imitators of God, as beloved children"* (Ephesians 5:1). We were spiritual widows until Christ, our bridegroom, loved us and gave Himself for us; we were sojourners, wondering aimlessly until Christ saved us; we were orphans, until God the Father adopted us and made us brothers and sisters of our elder brother, Christ. Consequently, to love these three groups of people is to demonstrate the love of God in a powerful way.

CONVICTION 3:
GOD COMMANDS HIS PEOPLE TO SHARE HIS CONCERN FOR THE FATHERLESS.

In Isaiah, God rebukes the religious who have large worship services but have denied the act of caring for the widow and the orphan. He says:

> *Learn to do good; seek justice, correct oppression; bring justice*
> *to the fatherless, plead the widow's cause.*
>
> —Isaiah 1:17–18

In Deuteronomy, God gave instructions to Israel about giving appropriate justice and sufficient food for the sojourner, fatherless, and widowed. Why? Because they were once slaves in Egypt before God rescued them. They too were to show the rescuing love of God.

> *"You shall not pervert the justice due to the sojourner or to the*
> *fatherless, or take a widow's garment in pledge, but you shall*
> *remember that you were a slave in Egypt and the Lord your God*
> *redeemed you from there; therefore I command you to do this.*
> *When you reap your harvest in your field and forget a sheaf*
> *in the field, you shall not go back to get it.*
> *It shall be for the sojourner, the fatherless, and the widow,*
> *that the Lord your God may bless you in all the work of your hands.*
> *When you beat your olive trees, you shall not go over them again.*
> *It shall be for the sojourner, the fatherless, and the widow. When you*
> *gather the grapes of your vineyard, you shall not strip it afterward.*
> *It shall be for the sojourner, the fatherless, and the widow.*
> *You shall remember that you were a slave in the land of Egypt;*
> *therefore I command you to do this."*
>
> —Deuteronomy 24:17–22

As we will see, God's moral demands about caring for the orphan are consistent with the teaching of the New Testament also.

In Psalm 82, God tells Israel to give justice to those who have no voice. Here we find one of the purposes of influence: to speak up for those who have no influence. The psalmist writes:

> *Give justice to the weak and the fatherless; maintain the right of the*
> *afflicted and the destitute. Rescue the weak and the needy;*
> *deliver them from the hand of the wicked.*
>
> —Psalm 82:3–4

Likewise, in Proverbs 31, a godly mother speaks to her kingly son saying:

> *Open your mouth, judge righteously,*
> *defend the rights of the poor and needy.*
>
> —Proverbs 31:9

We seldom hear about the great needs of the poor and the orphan because we don't hear them. They don't speak at conferences. We don't see them on broadcast news. This makes the situation worse. We actually can live comfortably and ignore them as if they don't exist. But they do exist! And God's people are called to defend, protect, and deliver them from the oppressors.

RESPONDING TO JAMES 1:27

A couple of years ago, this Scripture had a profound impact on the church where I was preaching. I simply read, explained, and applied this verse:

> *Religion that is pure and undefiled before God, the Father, is this:*
> *to visit orphans and widows in their affliction, and to keep*
> *oneself unstained from the world.*
>
> —James 1:27

In response to God's Word, a few women initiated a new ministry for prospective adoptive parents called Abba Father Ministry. The goal of the ministry is to help parents adopt children by granting financial assistance. In addition to this ministry, I've watched men and women respond to God's clear instruction in James in many other God-reflecting ways. You will read some of their stories later in the book. And this verse had such an impact on my wife and me that we named our son James.

The Bible's James says that true "religion" involves compassionate caring for the orphan. That's not all that's involved, but it's a good test for believers. I'll be the first to say that I don't like the word *religion*. And in the New Testament it's usually used as a pejorative term (Acts 26:5; Colossians 2:18). But here James uses the term positively. He calls this religion *"faith in our Lord Jesus Christ"* in the next verse (James 2:1). The Pharisees were experts at dead religion. Jesus told them that they were hypocrites because they neglected the *"weightier matters of . . . justice and mercy and faithfulness"* (Matthew 23:23). Their worship was nothing but "rules taught by men" (Matthew 15:9). They had external rituals, but missed the real heart of true religion. They were guilty of the sin of *omission*; that is, failing to do God's commands.

Acceptable religion obeys God's command to care practically for those in need. New Testament scholar Douglas Moo summarizes this in "The Letter of James" in *The Pillar New Testament Commentary:*

> One test of pure religion, therefore, is the degree to which we extend aid to the "helpless" in our world—whether they be widows and orphans, immigrants trying to adjust to a new life, impoverished third-world dwellers, the handicapped, or the homeless.

Another important word in James 1:27 is *visit*. James says that faithful Christianity involves the "visiting" of orphans. The original meaning for the word, *episkeptesthai*, means more than dropping by for a donut. It has to do with personal touch and involvement. It means to care for others, exercising oversight on their behalf and helping them in their need. It is from the same root as *episkipos*, which means "overseer" (sometimes translated as "bishop"). James is basically saying to be a shepherd to the orphan

This powerful term is used in the Bible frequently of God's visiting His people to redeem and encourage them, particularly during pivotal stages of history with the arrival of key redemptive leaders, ultimately seen in the birth of Christ (See Genesis 21:1; 50:24; Exodus 3:16, 4:31, Ruth 1:6; Luke 1:68, 78, 7:16; Acts 7:23; 15:14).

We should note that when God "visited" His people, He did not just send a check! He came personally to the aid of His people. We shouldn't be content with just sending money either. Instead, we should come to the aid of orphans in order to reflect, "This is what God is like!" We show the world what the Father is like by caring for those in need, which may be why James mentions "*God the father*" (James 1:27).

One beautiful example of showing God's nature to those in need is in Luke 7:16, with the story of Jesus raising the son of the widow of Nain. Jesus saw the widow and said with compassion, "*Do not weep*" (Luke 7:13). Then He raised the young man, and Luke writes, "*gave him to his mother*" (7:15). In other words, Jesus indicated, "This widow needs you." The response of the crowd? Awesome. They said, "*God has visited his people*" (7:16). Jesus' actions were saying: "I am God, and this is what He is like." He visits, saves, redeems, encourages, cares for—the orphan and widow. Disciples of Jesus will follow this example.

I encourage you to listen to how John Piper echoes this in his sermon, "Visiting Orphans in a World of AIDS and Abortion," available online at www.discoveringgod.org

What a vision for the Christian and the church! Let's reflect the redeeming nature of God's mercy by obediently caring for the orphan in radical Christ-honoring ways, thereby avoiding the hypocrisy of the Pharisees.

CONVICTION 4:
GOD IS PRO-ADOPTION.

Indeed, from the beginning of the Bible, we see God valuing children. As His imitators, we must avoid seeing children as a nuisance or a distraction, and see them as a blessing. Psalm 127 says, "*Blessed is the man* who fills his quiver *with them*" (Psalm 127:5; emphasis added). Notice how the English Standard Version translates this verse; it's *active*. In other words, *go fill your quiver* and be blessed!

God is not only pro-kids; He's also pro-adoption. Think of the number of people who were adopted in the Bible. In *God, Marriage, and Family*, author Andreas Kostenberger reminds us:

> *Dan and Naphtali, and later Ephraim and Manasseh, were adopted by Jacob (Gen. 30:1–13; 48:5); Moses was adopted by Pharaoh's daughter (Ex. 2:10); and Esther was adopted by Mordecai (Est. 2:7). . . .*
>
> *In the New Testament, the most prominent example is Jesus' adoption by Joseph, who served as his earthly father, participating in his naming (Matt. 1:25), presenting him in the temple (Luke 2:22–24), protecting him from danger by taking him and his mother to Egypt (Matt. 2:13–15), and by teaching him a trade (Matt. 13:55; Mark 6:3).*

Kostenberger concludes:

> *These biblical examples may serve as encouraging evidence for some married couples that the practice of adoption has honorable biblical precedent. Together, with the metaphoric use of adoption in the New Testament [Rom. 8:15, 23; 9:4; Gal. 4:5; Eph. 1:5] . . . these passages*

show that adopted children are to be taken into a loving, intimate, and permanent context of a biblical marriage and family.

But not only are there positive biblical examples of adoption, there is also one other big reason we know God is pro-adoption: the gospel! The doctrine of adoption is at the heart of the gospel. Adoption was never plan B; it has always been plan A. It existed before the world existed. Paul wrote, *"In love, he predestined us for adoption as sons through Jesus Christ, according to the purpose of his will"* (Ephesians 1:4-5). God planned on the act of adoption before creation. In Piper's words, "adoption is greater than the universe."

Because we love the gospel, we love the doctrine of adoption; that is, the study of God's adoption of us (further explained in the next chapter). As theologian J. I. Packer asserts in *Knowing God*, "Adoption is the highest privilege that the gospel offers: higher even than justification. . . . To be right with God the Judge is a great thing, but to be loved and cared for by God the Father is greater."

Once we begin to see the glory of God's adoption of sinners as the highest privilege of the gospel, then our view of the adoption of kids changes dramatically. We get to demonstrate the gospel. Since God is pro-adoption, will you be? Historically, Christians have been.

They Will Know Us By Our Love

Faithful Christians throughout the years have displayed great mercy to the fatherless. They serve as inspiring examples for us today. These heroes also demonstrate that one identifiable mark of Christians throughout the generations has been their Christlike love.

Early Christians

The Apology of Aristides the Philosopher (translated by D. M. Kay) records the philosopher Aristides' description of the Christlike care of early believers as told to the Emperor Hadrian around the year A.D. 125. He said:

> *Further, if one or other of them have bondmen and bondwomen or children, through love towards them they persuade them to become Christians, and when they have done so, they call them brethren without distinction. They do not worship strange gods, and they go their way*

in all modesty and cheerfulness. Falsehood is not found among them;
and they love one another, and from widows they do not turn away their
esteem; and they deliver the orphan from him who treats him harshly.
And he, who has, gives to him who has not, without boasting. And when
they see a stranger, they take him in to their homes and rejoice over him
as a very brother; for they do not call them brethren after the flesh, but
brethren after the spirit and in God. And whenever one of their poor
passes from the world, each one of them according to his ability gives
heed to him and carefully sees to his burial. And if they hear that one
of their number is imprisoned or afflicted on account of the name of
their Messiah, all of them anxiously minister to his necessity, and if it
is possible to redeem him they set him free. And if there is among them
any that is poor and needy, and if they have no spare food, they fast."

Notice that among the acts of mercy listed by Aristides was "delivering the orphan from him who treats him harshly." This inspiring document demonstrates the distinct acts of compassion that separated God's people from others in the culture, illustrating Jesus' words, *"By this all people will know that you are my disciples, if you have love for one another"* (John 13:35).

George Whitefield

One of the primary preachers of the Great Awakening in America in the 1740s was George Whitefield. Whitefield is most known for his preaching on the new birth. His oratory was so powerful that he attracted people who didn't believe in his message, such as Benjamin Franklin and David Hume. Whitefield traveled all over America and Britain preaching the gospel and saw amazing results.

After reading a biography of Whitefield, I was surprised by his great love for building an orphanage in Georgia. In fact, when he preached to throngs of people he regularly took up an offering for the orphanage! When was the last time you saw an evangelist pleading with people after the sermon to give for the cause of the fatherless?

The name of the orphanage was Bethesda, or House of Mercy. It was founded near Savannah in 1740. Arnold Dallimore writes in his biography of Whitefield, "The publicity Whitefield gave to the Orphan House evoked new interest in general efforts to assist the needy and aroused other men to undertake endeavors for the underprivileged." May God raise up more passionate evangelists and zealous advocates for the fatherless like Whitefield!

CHARLES SPURGEON

My historical hero is the incomparable Baptist preacher-pastor, Charles Spurgeon. He's most known for his incredible amount of books still in print, many of which include his sermons preached at the Tabernacle in London, where he began a 38-year pastorate beginning in 1854. While some know that Spurgeon also started a college, fewer know that he also started an orphanage.

Arnold Dallimore, in his biography of Spurgeon, records that in a prayer meeting in 1866, Spurgeon said, "Dear friends, we are a huge church, and should be doing more for the Lord in this great city. I want us, tonight, to ask Him to *send us some new work*; and if we need money to carry it on, let us pray that *the means also may be sent*." After some providential experiences, conversations, and generous gifts, the people set out to build an orphanage (in addition to the existing almshouses previously built for widows).

The buildings were joined together, forming a continuous row and each home included 14 boys under the care of a matron who acted as a mother. They were taught Christian education, sport, and individuality. Ten years after the boys' side was finished, a similar building was constructed for girls. The children thronged to Spurgeon, and he spoke of the orphanage with great love in his sermons. These children came from all types of backgrounds, of all different ethnicities. Dallimore even notes that "from time to time some of the youngsters were converted and asked for baptism, and there were boys who, upon growing up, experienced the call of God, attended the Pastor's College, and went on into a life in the ministry."

Interestingly, Spurgeon spoke strongly to an agnostic who challenged Spurgeon's beliefs. He compared the failure of the unbeliever's social organizations to care for the needy with the works of evangelical Christianity, such as the orphanages. To end their conversation, Spurgeon paraphrased the triumphant cry of Elijah to the false prophets of his day, saying, "The God who answereth by Orphanages, Let Him Be God." In other words, Spurgeon believed that evangelicals gave witness to the true and living God by their care for and involvement with the poor and the orphan.

GEORGE MULLER

George Muller lived in the 1800s and is in fact known for his work in orphanages in Bristol, England. He's surely the most famous orphanage founder in the world. In 1836, the first orphanage opened just seven weeks after he announced to the church his plans to build it. He eventually built five orphan houses before he died at age 92.

According to Muller biographers Janet and Geoff Benge, Muller is particularly well known for his practice of prayer and his experience of God's providence in caring for the children. On one particular occasion, one of the orphanages had nothing to feed the 300 children in the orphanage. Muller prayed, "Dear God, we thank You for what You are going to give us to eat. Amen." Muller looked up and smiled at the children. He said, "You may be seated." No sooner did the kids sit down did they hear a knock at the door. A baker stood in the doorway with delicious smelling bread. The baker said, "Mr. Muller, I couldn't sleep last night. I keep thinking that somehow you would need bread this morning . . . so I got up and made three batches for you. I hope you can use it." Soon, there was another knock at the door. This time it was the milkman. He said, "I'm needing a little help, if you could, sir. The wheel on my cart is broken, right outside your establishment. I'll have to lighten my load before I can fix it. There's ten full cans of milk on it. Can you use them?" He looked at the children and said, "Free of charge, of course." There was enough milk for every child to have a mug full with more leftover for lunch. God provided bread and milk for the children on this day and continued to provide for this faithful leader's ministry.

Though he never asked for funds, numerous individuals supported his work. He was a living illustration of living by faith in the living God. It is estimated that Muller helped care for over 10,000 children in his lifetime. In addition, Muller distributed Bibles, preached his whole life, served as pastor in one church for 66 years (and refused a salary!), and helped missionaries such as Hudson Taylor.

We could go on. Countless Christians through the years have actively helped the fatherless through various forms of orphan care, such as financial assistance, regular visitations, building orphanages, adoptions, rescuing oppressed children, and foster care. They have obeyed the biblical texts on this matter.

When will the world know we are Jesus' disciples? When we speak about the Savior *and* show the love of the Savior.

— TM

AN ADOPTION STORY—LEE AND BARBARA DRAKE

*B*eing married to an OBGYN, I had it all planned out. We would get pregnant, Lee would have all the answers to my questions, and one of his colleagues would deliver our baby (free of charge, I might add). Well, I have never been pregnant, Lee did not have all the answers, and fertility treatments were not cheap! The doctors diagnosed us with unexplained infertility. We tried many different methods over the course of five years without success. Not having children was not an option for us so we turned to adoption. After mounds of paperwork and many months of waiting, we received a phone call from our agency…we had a boy! We were ecstatic! The first time we laid eyes on him we understood why we couldn't get pregnant…God had a different plan for us. Seventeen months after our son's adoption we decided to adopt again, this time through the international route. We were off to China to adopt our daughter. What a joy! We now had a boy and a girl, the best of both worlds. What more could we want?

We have now raised our children for 15 years. It has been and continues to be the best and hardest job we've ever had. We enjoy our children and can't imagine our life without them. However, envisioning our children moving out on their own and us approaching retirement had begun to seem appealing. But, once again, God had other plans. In the summer of 2009 Lee and I visited an orphan hosting camp. There were six children here from Ukraine. We fell in love with all of them! One Sunday after church, Lee was going over the first chapter of James (he was trying to memorize the entire book of James). It was the same Sunday that the kids from Ukraine visited our church. Lee was on James 1:27; *"religion that God our Father accepts pure and faultless is this: to look after orphans and widows in their distress and to keep oneself from being polluted by the world"* (NIV). He called me on the phone from his car and said listen to this…and then read James 1:27. He said, "What do you think that means to us?" I quickly said, "I think that means we are going to have a couple more kids!" As I write this we are waiting to travel to Ukraine to adopt three more teenage boys. Lee and I don't know what God has in store for us, but we look forward to the joys and heartaches of raising more children. Our prayer for each one of our children is that they come to know Jesus Christ and have a personal relationship with Him. I am always asking my kids, "How did God pick out the most perfect children for us?" and they reply, "I don't know, but he just did!"

— LDB

Adoption is not just about couples who want children— or who want more children. Adoption is about an entire culture within our churches, a culture that sees adoption as part of our Great Commission mandate and as a sign of the gospel itself.

—Russell D. Moore, *Adopted for Life*

4

HOW DO YOU LEAD A CHURCH TO CARE FOR THE FATHERLESS?

*T*he church of Jesus Christ is the most powerful force in the world. It has the power of the Holy Spirit, the best news in the world, financial wealth, a multitude of troops, access to technology, and for the first time in history, the ability to travel to anywhere in the world in a day or two. Indeed, the church can turn the world upside down by acts of mercy and the proclamation of the good news. Orphan care and adoption is part of this redemptive mission. The question for us as individual Christians and as Christ's body is:

Will we settle for a safe, comfortable religion or will we use these recourses for the good of the world and the glory of Christ?

The purpose of this chapter is to identify and describe several ways the church, leaders in general, and pastors in particular, can influence the church to use God's resources to do gospel-centered orphan care. Feel free to discuss other innovative ideas on this matter, but here are a few basic, simple, and life-changing things to move the church to a greater living faith that manifests itself in manifold acts of mercy.

We have a dream of seeing hundreds of adopted children from around the globe in local churches. We can see adoptive families filled with children from all nations gathered together, as a little glimpse of heaven, smiling for photographs. We also have a dream of seeing regular church members, young and old alike, involved in orphan ministries such as orphan-hosting programs, adoption funding, oversees trips to orphanages and so forth. What's your dream for your local ministry? How do we turn these dreams into realities?

A CULTURE OF ORPHAN CARE

To see these types of dreams come to life in the local church, we believe the goal is to develop a culture of orphan care—a church where the spirit of God's heart for the fatherless permeates the church with unmistakable power and clarity.

Starbucks has shown us about creating a culture. When you go into Starbucks, you know that they are all about coffee. They have the marketing, products, merchandise, and personnel—and even their own language. They have people talking about coffee. The place smells like coffee, and people sit down, take a sip, and talk about . . . coffee.

Similarly, a church with an orphan care culture will have ministries, teams, printed materials, media, common language, Bible studies, and regular discussions on the topic. They will pray about orphan care in public and private, develop fellowship groups to discuss it, and host events to bring awareness about it. They will celebrate with couples that adopt. They will support the orphan ministries with passion. The church will have *an aroma of Christ's love for the fatherless.*

In other words, the church is disinterested in orphan care being a department relegated to the few who feel sorry for kids. Rather, the whole church is interested in caring for as many orphans as the body can care about because individuals see this as a part of the Great Commandment and Great Commission, which Jesus did not relegate to a select few but to every disciple.

Spiritual leaders should do three great things to develop a culture of orphan care:

1. lead with the Word,
2. lead by example, and
3. lead with a simple plan.

LEAD WITH THE WORD

*T*he first place to begin with promoting a biblical view of adoption and orphan care is by addressing the matter with clear and compelling biblical instruction. Many ministry emphases in the local church begin with the pastor's preaching. But that shouldn't be just because he's the "leader" but because he's teaching the *Bible*! As evangelical Christians, we live under the Word, submitting to its *authority*. Therefore, for a Christian to be persuaded about any aspect of the Christian life, he or she should want to see it first and foremost from the Scriptures.

The role of the preacher is to do just that—to declare, "Thus says the Lord" by opening the Scriptures, teaching the Scriptures and applying them to the lives of the hearers. Those who teach in other contexts in the church (such as in small groups) should also seek to guide the people through the Word. When it comes to the subject of orphan care, we need to give the hearers the clear teaching of Scripture regarding adoption and orphan care by instructing them to be doers of the Word, not hearers only (James 1:22–27).

Further, the leader's biblical *application* in preaching and teaching should call people's attention to the need for orphan care *specifically* as he or she speaks on *general* subjects of the Christian life such as: loving our neighbors, missions, caring for the poor, hospitality, or the family. The congregation should not only hear about adoption and orphan care when a passage is solely devoted to it. To cast a biblical vision that sinks into the minds of the people, it needs to be mentioned

> Adoption and orphan care should appear in sermons regularly.

regularly. Something about adoption and orphan care should appear in sermons regularly, if the church is going to create a culture of orphan care. Every teacher needs to refer regularly to the subject by means of application.

In addition, church study should address particular subjects in detail in order to instruct and inspire believers. Every church should strongly consider studying the doctrine of adoption. Perhaps no other issue in the Scriptures will motivate people to radical, adopting love like seeing the details of God's adoption of us through Jesus Christ. J. I. Packer in his book *Knowing God* writes, "Our understanding of Christianity cannot be better than our grasp of adoption." Teaching on adoption then will have a double effect; it will show the nature of salvation, and it will inspire us to live out the mercy of God by actually adopting and caring for orphans.

Of course, any series through books like Romans, Ephesians, and Galatians will force the pastor/teachers to take up the subject of adoption. Consider a biblical theological study of adoption, instead of a verse-by-verse, book-by-book study, and a few weeks focusing solely on those passages that deal with adoption in these particular books (like Ephesians 1:3–14; Galatians 4:4–7; and Romans 8:12–39).

Another idea is a series on particular doctrines *related* to God's adoption of us. Some of the doctrines that naturally relate to God's grace in adoption include:

1. the love of God;
2. the foundation for Christian hope;
3. the ministry of the Spirit;
4. the motives for holiness;
5. the nature of assurance of salvation;
6. the family of God;
7. prayer;
8. heaven.

All of these (and more) touch on being sons and daughters of God.

Those who minister the Word might also consider doing a series considering the subject of the *fatherhood* of God, as well. The Bible speaks of God's fatherhood frequently in terms of Christian discipleship, as illustrated in the Sermon on Mount (Matthew 5:16, 44*a*, 45*a*; 6:4*b*, 9*a*, 32*a*). By pointing to the nature of God the Father, hopefully people will begin to see the type of love we are called to imitate (Ephesians 5:1–2).

In addition to the continual referencing of adoption and orphan care in the course of weekly preaching and teaching, and the focused attention of preaching series of sermons like those mentioned, the pastor-teacher could also think about doing an annual sermon on the subject of the fatherless. For example, on Father's Day, is there a better subject to turn people's eyes toward than to see the heavenly Father whose love abides forever? In a world in which children are abandoned, sold, and killed, the Father of glory remains with us forever. And the more daddies are like the heavenly Father, the better daddies they will be.

Another annual focus could be Orphan Sunday, which recently became a recognized day in many churches. Consider carving out this particular day to caste vision, begin a series, or simply to preach and teach on the subject and utilize the video options, and other tools at www.orphansunday.org. Though preaching and teaching on this subject once a year is not enough for the vision to spread.

Indeed, the preacher-teacher is an influencer. If you are a pastor, don't underestimate the power of opening up the Word, teaching the people, and asking questions like:

> *Would you begin to pray about your role for caring for the fatherless?*
> *Will you and your spouse pray for the next month about adopting?*
> *If you are too old to adopt, would you consider supporting one of our families who is trying to adopt?*

You don't have to have massive programs for developing an orphan care culture; you simply need to teach the Bible and influence individual believers to answer personal, direct, and challenging questions. And then keep on teaching and emphasizing orphan care throughout the church.

LEAD BY EXAMPLE

*L*eaders must embody the vision they proclaim. As pastors, we know we must put the vision on display by personal example or else we're hypocrites of the worst kind. The model of leadership taught by Jesus and reinforced in the rest of the New Testament is clearly *servant leadership*, not *top-down* leadership. Top-down leadership barks orders and abuses authority. Jesus, however, showed His disciples what it looked like to love the unlovable, what it looked like to wash feet, and what it looked like to make sacrifices for the good of others. His teaching *explained* the vision, but His personal life *demonstrated* the vision. Both components are essential for persuading others to follow a dream.

By this, we don't mean that every pastor-leader must adopt. Several respected pastors haven't actually adopted, but still set an incredible example for caring for orphans by advocacy, support, developing ministries, equipping others, and so on. Some pastors want to adopt or are waiting to adopt. Some actually have adopted. We're not basing "leading by example" on whether or not a pastor has adopted kids, but whether or not leaders are setting an example of servant leadership in the multiple ways possible. A few pastors whom we know exemplify concern for orphans include these individuals:

A search for adoption on Dr. John Piper's Web site, www.desiringgod.org, yields some 40 pages of resources, such as sermons, letters, blog posts, and more about God's adoption of us and our role to reflect God's mercy.

Not only has Piper written and preached about it, but he's also experienced the wonder of adoption. He and his wife, Noël, had four biological sons before the Lord led them to adopt a daughter when he was in his 50s! Reflecting on it in an interview in 2009, Piper said:

> *I do think children are an amazing blessing from the Lord. I have 5, and I'm glad I have 5 kids. And if I had to do it over again, I would have 5 plus. I would start adopting earlier probably. We had 4 of the biological kind and then Talitha, and we waited perhaps too long to have Talitha (Noël would say we did).*

Noël tells of how they initially planned on adopting two children and having two biological children, but as time wore on, the conversations about adoption never materialized into more than conversation between spouses. One day, though, the phone rang and a woman told Noël that they had a baby girl in Georgia that she felt was perfect for her. Noël immediately wished to adopt, but she knew that this could not be something that one parent wholeheartedly embraced and the other didn't. As their four boys grew up and moved out of the house, Dr. Piper was excited about having the house empty and devoting himself to writing books and going to the missions field, or doing whatever the Lord led him to do. Noël really wanted to adopt this little girl, though. She and Dr. Piper began to discuss and pray their way through the thought of adoption. Eventually, Dr. Piper warmed to the idea of adoption, and the Lord led him to fully embrace and love this concept of adoption. Soon thereafter, he presented his wife with a paper that he had written to her fully embracing the adoption of their daughter!

Rick Warren has been a voice for social issues all over the globe, and so has his wife, Kay. Pastor Warren has developed the PEACE Plan, which stands for "Preach Reconciliation," "Equip Leaders," "Assist the Poor," "Care for the Sick," and "Educate the Next Generation." At a recent event, the church's leader of the PEACE Plan said that a common thread throughout each of these actions is a "concern for orphans." I'm amazed by the fact that Saddleback has been to every country involved in missions and displays their concern for orphans in several of those nations.

In one sermon in the fall of 2009, Pastor Warren called for 500 Saddleback families to adopt children! The church also hosts seminars, forums, and workshops that aid members in the work of planning and preparing for an adoption and becoming foster parents. The church continues to care for the fatherless through the exemplary leadership of Pastor Warren.

Our friend, David Platt, senior pastor of the Church at Brook Hills in Birmingham, Alabama, leads his church by example also. In one year, his church cut expenses in the final months to care for those with urgent physical and spiritual needs. One particular focus of this movement has been caring for the fatherless. Brook Hills already had a strong adoption emphasis. In fact, David and his wife, Heather, had adopted a young boy from Kazakhstan and were in the process of adopting more children. But during this shift of resources, David and the church began emphasizing the importance of *foster care* also. They made the following commitment:

> *In obedience to Scripture, we have decided that we can not and will not sit idly by while children are in need of a home to care and provide for their deepest needs in difficult times, whether that is for a short time or for a lifetime. We long to show God's love in metro Birmingham in a way that not only serves the children around us but ultimately honors the Father to the fatherless (Psalm 68:5). As a result, we have dedicated ourselves to recruiting and raising up individuals and families to provide for all of the foster care and adoption needs in our county.*

David spoke at a conference hosted by another great example: Russell Moore. Dr. Moore is a theologian and preaching pastor and author, who adopted children from Russia recently. Much of Dr. Moore's itinerant preaching schedule has been set aside for preaching on orphan care and challenging the church to act on behalf of the fatherless. Some now refer to Dr. Moore as "the adoption guy."

In the church where Dr. Moore serves as preaching pastor, Highview Baptist Church, Louisville, Kentucky, the senior pastor, Kevin Ezell, has also adopted on several different occasions! Pastor Ezell recently led an initiative at his denomination's convention to raise a fund for pastors who want to adopt. Following a sermon preached by Dr. Moore, Ezell announced that some scholarships were available for potential candidates and the response from pastors was overwhelming. Many pastors displayed a desire to adopt.

We could go on with this list. The point is that leaders like these are changing churches not only by preaching on the subject, but also by personal example. And it's not pastors alone. Bible fellowship teachers, ministers of youth, and other faithful servant leaders are providing an example of what it looks like to embody the vision.

LEAD WITH A SIMPLE PLAN

*E*xposing the truth of the Scriptures regarding the fatherless and illustrating those truths by personal example should be followed up with a workable strategy for God's people. Here's where the vision often loses momentum. If the people don't understand some practical steps for engaging the dream, they will grow weary or discouraged and possibly even disengage from the vision itself.

Orphan-care ministry is no different than most other ministries in the church. To begin, servant leaders can:

Show how orphan care is aligned with the church's overall vision and then, develop ministries that flesh out the vision.

Next, equip people through training programs, events, and ongoing resources.

Reflect the vision and subsequent orphan ministries in the budget.

As the ministries develop, celebrate and evaluate constantly. Finally, keep influencing the influencers in your church through personal relationships.

1. ALIGN WITH THE CHURCH'S OVERALL VISION AND VALUES

The vision and values of orphan care should fall in line with the biblical vision of the church as a whole. What's your church's vision? Whatever way it's articulated should have to do with the Great Commission and the Great Commandment expressed in the New Testament. Orphan care is a part (not the whole) of this vision of making disciples of all nations and loving our neighbors as ourselves. The leader needs to make sure that individual members know that orphan care is not a "maverick ministry" running off on its own, as something "else" the church does; it as a part of the big picture.

2. DEVELOP MINISTRIES THAT PUT FEET TO THE VISION

If your vision is to change the lives of orphans for the glory of Christ, then you need to consider how people can accomplish this. Not everyone will adopt. Some will. Some can offer assistance in other ways.

Here are a few ideas. First, consider doing an adoption fund at your church (see chap. 6). Second, contact your local foster-care system and see how your church can assist them (see chap. 7). Third, consider partnering with an overseas orphanage and set up an orphan-hosting program (see chap. 9).

Fourth, consider adopting an international orphanage that is not open to adoptions. You may support them by sending teams to love and care for the kids. Others might go help build a facility. You might consider having members sponsor these kids and send them gifts on special occasions. I've experienced the great joy of serving kids in unadoptable areas. I've also seen church members showing me their letters and pictures that come from these children. They've learned to love and support and pray from a distance. And it's no small thing to do this.

> Human trafficking generates more than $12 billion a year for those who sell human lives into slavery and sexual bondage.

Finally, consider doing something with child trafficking. See the resources in the Appendix for helps and examples. This evil enterprise of human trafficking generates more than $12 billion a year for those who sell human lives into slavery and sexual bondage. Nearly 2 million children are abused in this wicked industry. And of course, the global sex trade perpetuates the problem of AIDS, as well. The church may consider developing its own branch of orphan ministry that looks solely at this issue. You could host seminars, provide advocacy training, bring awareness of the problem and various events, participate in legal processes, pray for particular groups that are devoted to this cause, provide literature to people who don't understand the issue, or even partner with an existing agency and let them speak and provide training at your church.

Look around in your own area. What can you do? What ministries need to be developed? Each church is different. Each church's orphan ministries will also look different.

3. Equip People Through Training

After developing the ministries, it's essential that people have training. The church leaders don't always have the needed expertise to do particular forms of training for things like foster care, but one could easily invite someone to discuss it in seminar fashion. One idea would be to adopt a Sunday to talk about orphan care from the pulpit (Father's Day or Orphan Sunday, perhaps), and then provide training seminars during the afternoon on specific ministries. Or, consider making a weekend about orphan care, in which you have a keynote speaker on Friday night, seminars on Saturday, and then address the topic from the pulpit on Sunday.

We recently decided to split our traditional Wednesday night prayer meeting in half. One group now sings hymns, has a Bible study, and prays for the needs of the church. The new gathering is devoted to practical training in the missional activities in which we are engaged: church planting, world evangelization, aid for the poor and the sick, care for the orphan and the oppressed, and equipping leaders. After hearing the vision and the big picture from the pulpit, this smaller gathering is important because people always have follow-up questions and need dialogue. Here, questions are answered, stories about things such as orphan care are shared, and the nuts and bolts of these ministries are explained. We simply took a night in which people were already coming to church and repurposed it around our vision and focused on actual equipping.

You may also decide to take your leaders to churches where orphan care is being done well through a local church. If you want to start an orphan-hosting program, then it would be a great idea to take your leaders and visit a church that's doing it well. Training for fighting human trafficking, will almost have to be done by those who work there full-time because of the legal issues related and the number of unknowns, although there are resources available at places like www.ijm.org where you'll find things like fact sheets, prayer guides, and ways to get involved. But again, I think it's wise and good to teach on the theological issues of this matter from the pulpit and then provide the practical training by the experts at the same time.

> Many people will not know you're serious about something until it's in the budget.

One means of ongoing training is providing resources. The easiest way to do this is with a blog, where you devote attention to posting articles, videos, books, and other commentary on the orphan care. You might also consider having orphan-care books available to read or purchase. Remember to keep your information fresh and profitable.

4. REFLECT YOUR VALUES IN THE BUDGET

Many people will not know you're serious about something until it's in the budget. Of course, you can do orphan ministry with a limited budget, but I think you should always reflect what you are serious about by putting your money where your mouth is.

Maybe you want to start by simply adopting an orphanage of children not available for adoption. We recently adopted an orphanage in Asia full of precious children and put about $6,000 in the budget, which basically covered half the cost of living for the entire orphanage. We then took up additional offerings at VBS for the same orphanage, and eventually were able to send more than $10,000 to this orphanage. You will be amazed at how far the dollar goes in particular countries. You might also consider adding line items for orphan hosting, visits to orphanages, or missions trips that will serve in local and global orphanages. As time goes on, hopefully these dollar amounts can increase. Start small if you have to and then add more dollars as you can.

5. EVALUATE AND CELEBRATE REGULARLY

Ministries must always engage in evaluation. Here are three simple, effective questions to ask about every ministry in a church:

1. What needs to be added?
2. What needs tweaking?
3. What needs to be done away with?

When evaluations are finished, assignments need to be made and deadlines given. If changes are made, then they are to be communicated to the church.

It is surprising how little evaluation happens in the church. Some are even bothered by asking probing questions. Yet leaders must evaluate. Evaluation will help keep ministries in alignment with the church's whole vision, and are a means for providing affirmation, and eliciting improvement.

At times in the evaluation you may decide that you want to go for something new, like perhaps a new ministry. To distinguish between a "prudent risk" and a "wild-eyed gamble," Larry Osborne, writing an assessment tool for *Christianity Today*'s buildingchurchleaders.com, suggests that you ask the following questions:

- "Who else has done it?" This will help you see potential dangers.
- "How bad can it get? If you can't live with the worst-case scenario, it's seldom a risk worth taking.
- "Can we give it a trial run?" This will keep you from a devastatingly dumb move. You'll just be a bit discouraged if it doesn't work.
- "How much room do we have for error?". . . Do you already have the trust of others and deep relationships?
- "How clearly has God spoken?" We know God has spoken on orphan care in the Bible. But how do you think God is leading you to apply His Word in your context?

The church should also be informed of the wonderful stories of adoption and orphan ministry, to celebrate the great stories of God's grace. Again, the blog is a wonderful place for this. My wife has people from all over the globe viewing her blog (www.betheglory.blogspot.com) as she writes about God's mercy over our family. If you do a newsletter, or email update, make sure to include some first-person testimonies. Celebrate the stories from the pulpit, if possible, or show videos of families who've adopted and mercy ministries that are happening that are spreading joy and truth to orphans.

I've shared the story of my sister adopting five kids from Ethiopia repeatedly. I've prayed for folks like Adam and Jill publicly, while they were in Uganda adopting two kids. I've shown pictures of my wife in East Asia on a trip to fight against child trafficking. We've featured families in our newsletter, like Glen and Lisa who adopted two teenagers after participating in an orphan-hosting program. We've rejoiced at the return of families publicly, like Jim Bob and Crystal who adopted two teenagers in Ukraine. I've mentioned the Mixons, the Yearwoods, the Williamsons, and many more who've adopted

> I've accomplished the work that you gave me to do.

from our church. We've hosted speakers, like Randy Hall, who shared his experience of adopting several kids! We're praying for others in the adoption process presently. We've shown videos of our teams in places like Nigeria, where precious children were singing praise songs. We try to keep telling the stories. There's no need for a massive program to influence people; fanning the flame through personal testimonies and real life stories provides encouragement and incentive to others who are wondering if they can really do it.

6. KEEP INFLUENCING THE INFLUENCERS

Local churches may need better assimilation, organization, and strategic development. In Acts 6, the early church grew and the needs multiplied. They had to reassess things and restructure. The church will always need to be worked on because it is not really an organization but an *organism*—it's constantly growing and developing. Besides, the church is full of volunteers. Trying to inspire volunteers is a challenge!

So, as long as we're in ministry, we will be "building the plane while we're trying to fly it!" Our encouragement is this: Don't let a lack of superb organization keep you from caring for the millions of existing orphans as best as you can. You can do something.

How? You can care for orphans in any size church by remembering the power of individual influence. You have people in your church who influence numbers of people. You need to identify them, build relationships with them, instruct and inspire them and then urge them to spread the vision.

What did Jesus do to transform the world? To ask it another way, when Jesus prayed in John 17:4, "I've accomplished the work that you gave me to do," what was that *work*? In the rest of that prayer, Jesus mentioned . . . people. Specifically, He referred to His disciples. These disciples were His work. He taught them, lived among them, loved them, modeled the faith before them, and then commissioned them to make more followers. In John 17, Jesus never mentioned great sermons. He didn't even mention His miracles. He mentioned His disciples. What was result of His time with these influencers? They "*turned the world upside down*" (Acts 17:6).

A crucial component of leadership is the development of personal mentoring relationships with potentially influential leaders. If you want to turn the world upside down, invest in disciples and empower them to spread the vision.

Think about this. The most powerful means of advertising today is still word of mouth. You can change a church by structure partially. And you can also change it by the power of influencers embodying and sharing the dream, as well. As Ed Keller and Jon Berry say in *The Influentials*, "One American in ten tells the other nine how to vote, where to eat, and what to buy." Find these "ones," and help him or her spread their influence for the sake of the fatherless for the glory of Christ.

ORPHAN CARE IS WARFARE

*T*he church of Jesus Christ is the most powerful force in the world. But that doesn't mean there isn't opposition. If fulfilling the Great Commission and the Great Commandment involves spiritual warfare (which it does), and adoption and orphan care are part of the Great Commission and Great Commandment (which they are), that leads to this conclusion: orphan care is warfare.

Satan is a thief, a liar, a murderer, and a deceiver. He doesn't want us to do God's mission. He has many schemes for attack. We should expect him to be opposed to what I've mentioned in this chapter. That means that adoption and orphan care requires serious prayer, a reliance on God's power, and a steadfast faith in the promises of God.

You can expect opposition from the inside and the outside. From the outside, you will discover that many people are against you. Just remember there is something deeper going on other than what you see on the surface. Have you ever wondered why it is that there are so many fatherless children in the world? This is a spiritual matter. The world is not as it should be because of the fall. And why is it so hard to adopt? Could it be that there are spiritual forces involved? We aren't just dealing with ineffective governmental systems, we are engaging in spiritual war. You will face numerous trials in the adoption and orphan care journey, both in country and out of country. "Put on the whole armor or God, that you may be able to stand against the schemes of the devil" (Ephesians 6:11).

Spiritual warfare also comes from the outside through the media. Recently some terrible news has spread about adoption and awful movies have been displayed. Don't be surprised by this. As our level of obedience to God increases, so will the attack of the enemy. A counter movement to this orphan care movement is sure to exist. But be encouraged. *"He who is in you is greater than he who is in the world"* (1 John 4:4). And *"If God is for us, who can be against us?"* (Romans 8:31).

From the inside, you will encounter opposition, also. How does this come? It will come most painfully and perhaps most surprisingly from your own family. They may question you, criticize you, or even stand in opposition to you. Transracial adoptions will bring many forms of attack. People will ask questions. Some in the church will mock you or even reject your commitment. But remember that even though Jesus never promised that following Him would be easy, He did promise to go with us (Matthew 28:20). Therefore, the place to begin and continue in leading a church to do orphan care is on our knees, asking for God's strength to be made perfect in our weakness.

— TM

AN ADOPTION STORY—PAGE AND ASHLEY BROOKS

For many couples, the choice to adopt comes from various circumstances in life, normally from not being able to become pregnant. For us, adoption was always a part of our idea of a family even when we first married. If God blessed us with children by allowing pregnancy, that was fine too. Nevertheless, we knew from the very beginning that God had called us to adopt.

Three years into our marriage, God moved us to South Carolina from New Orleans. Neither of us wanted to move, but we knew it was the right decision. Two weeks after we moved out of New Orleans, Katrina hit the Gulf Coast. Both of us were grateful that God spared us the devastation, but we also felt that God had other reasons for us to move. After living in South Carolina for a year, we were presented with the opportunity to take a little boy into our home because his birth mom faced some legal trouble. We completed all of our paperwork for adoption (home study, background checks, etc.) and we did so in the record time of about two weeks. We also met an adoption lawyer who we found out later is the best adoption lawyer in the state. After an agonizing month of watching this little boy remain in foster care and the court system drag on and on we realized that this adoption was not going to happen. Eventually his mother was able to keep him, for which we were glad. Nevertheless, our hearts were broken, and we put adoption on hold for a little while.

> Nevertheless, our hearts were broken, and we put adoption on hold for a little while.

A few weeks later God prompted us to contact the adoption attorney we met in our previous adoption attempt to ask about their adoption process. The message we received back was the beginning of our faith journey. The social workers working with this adoption group said that if we had our paperwork ready (which we did from our previous attempt) we could be immediately put on a waiting list. The type of list was our choice. If we waited for a Caucasian baby it could be ten months to a year. If we wanted to put on the list for a "black baby" or "mixed-race baby," they could have one in our home tomorrow. We asked why there was such a difference in the wait time. The answer we were given broke our hearts. They said that "most white couples only want white babies" and "very few black couples" are adopting. We immediately knew what God was telling us to do. We knew that God wanted us to adopt the babies that others did not want. We were to adopt a mixed-raced or black child.

Two weeks after we turned in our paperwork, the lawyer's office called to tell us that a birth mom had chosen us to be the adoptive parents for her baby. We were given the privilege of meeting her a few days later and we fell in love with her. She was a second generation Puerto Rican from New York City. We did not know very much about the birth father other than he was black.

A week after the initial meeting with the birth mother, our first daughter, Karis Esperanza, was born. We were thrilled with her and immediately knew that God had done a mighty work in timing for Karis to be in our family. This adoption process, from the time we turned in our paperwork to the time she was in our home, was a little over a month. If we had not had our paperwork completed from our failed adoption attempt, Karis would not be in our home today.

Fourteen months after Karis was born, we felt God leading us to begin the adoption process a second time. We used the same adoption agency, but the only hitch was that we had moved back to New Orleans and were no longer living in the same state as our lawyer in South Carolina. It took us about a month to complete the paperwork needed. We turned in all the paperwork at the end of November. We prepared ourselves for the fact that every adoption is different and the likelihood of an adoption happening as quickly and smoothly as our last was very slim. We knew we wanted another mixed or black baby and we did not care whether the baby was a boy or girl. We thought there would be very little walking by faith with this adoption, but God had other plans.

> But God had other plans.

On New Year's Eve, our lawyer called us to tell us that a baby girl had been born and that the birth mom had chosen us to be her parents. They wanted to talk to us about this baby before we made plans to come get her. They told us that the baby had been born a "crack baby" and that the birth mom drank alcohol through the first part of her pregnancy and smoked through the entire pregnancy. She had failed her first APGAR test but had passed the second. She had a normal birth weight, but they could not be sure of the long-term effects of the drug and alcohol use.

We had completely different reactions to the news. Ashley was ready to jump in the car and go get the baby from the hospital. Because of her training in developmental psychology, she knew the possible ramifications of the drug and alcohol abuse, but she knew deep down that this baby was theirs no matter what. Page was a little more reluctant at first but, after spending some time in prayer, God reminded him of the type of children God had told us to adopt. We were to adopt the ones that no one else wanted. Within a day, they both knew that this baby girl was supposed to be in their home. Sixteen months to the day after Karis was born, Alethia Joy was born and added to our family. To this day she has shown no ramifications of the drug or alcohol abuse.

God has taught us so much through the adoption of these two precious girls. God has given us insights and an overwhelming love for another culture outside of our own. He has opened up numerous opportunities for us to share about how God wants to adopt each of us into His family. But probably the greatest blessing He has given us through our adoptions is the understanding that He desires for His church here on earth to look like the kingdom of heaven. He desires for every nation, tribe, and tongue to worship Him together as one, each and every time we come together on the Sabbath. We are so excited that God has given our family the opportunity to have a little bit of heaven here on earth as we choose to honor and glorify Him in a multiracial home each and every day.

— PBA

Vanya was abandoned at birth,
and spent the first 11 years of his life
in 4 different orphanages.

5

HOW DO YOU DO MISSIONS THROUGH ORPHANAGE FUNDING, PERSONNEL, AND TRAINING?

$\mathcal{I}$ will never forget my first trip into an orphanage. The sights and smells of that experience are indelibly imprinted on my mind. My wife and I were in Ternopil, Ukraine, to adopt our first son. To be honest, although I was certain God had us in that place at that time for His purpose, I was scared out of my mind.

We had just been though a ten-hour journey across Ukraine that seemed more like *Mister Toad's Wild Ride* than a well-planned, purposive trip to adopt. We were sleep-deprived and anxious, and as our taxi pulled up in front of the orphanage, nothing I saw did anything to relieve my anxiety. The hulking two-story orphanage building looked like something right out a movie set, and the scene that unfolded before us was something fit for a movie. The entire place, both inside and out, was huge and dark and impersonal looking. Outside in the courtyard were statues of what I imagine were characters from fairy tales. Not the kind of fairy tales that I would look forward to reading to my son. These characters were more like *Grimm's Fairy Tales* meets *Alice in Wonderland* meets *Charlie and the Chocolate Factory.*

Overall, everything seemed a little gray and depressed. After we had completed preliminary interviews with the orphanage director and head doctor, we were led down a long maze of cold, dark hallways. Seemingly, we passed an endless number of unused and unheated rooms. The lights, exposed lightbulb in sockets hanging from the ceiling by their wiring, were off presumably to conserve precious resources. After what seemed like a walk through a series of subterranean caverns, we were there! We had arrived at our soon-to-be son's "group." After waiting in a little unheated area outside the playroom, we were ushered into the playroom where we found 12 or 14 little toddlers and three workers. I remember being a little taken aback by what we found. I am not sure what I expected, but what I observed reminded me of several inner-city day-care facilities that I had visited while doing missions in the US.

The room was clean and well lit but spartan to be sure. The walls were block, and the floors were tile, and despite the playing children and their toys, it had the cold feel of an institution. The smell is something that I will never forget. It seems nearly everyone who has been in an Eastern European orphanage knows the smell. The odor reeks of both sterile and sour. The workers seemed pleasant and caring. I can imagine that they were a little overwhelmed or a little hardened by the difficulty of their task. Frankly, there were just too few ladies (and certainly no men) caring for too many children with far too few resources. I just wanted to cry. I wanted to take the full room of children home right then. I wanted to make a way for these children to know the warmth of a caring family.

I believe that if institutionalized children cannot be reunited with parents who will provide them with love, care, and a stable home, then adoption is the best solution for them. Sadly, as we have documented earlier, for many children who are growing up confined to an institution like the one described, adoption is not a likely option or maybe even an option at all. Many institutionalized children live in countries where in-country adoption is rare and intercountry adoption is prohibited. Still others are "social orphans" who are living in the orphanage but whose parents still retain their parental rights. Legally, these children are not recognized as abandoned, and hope remains that they may be reunited with their families at some point in the future.

The church must not forget these children or allow them to slip through the cracks. We must be active in devising ministry strategies to share the love and nurture of Christ with them and to improve their lives as they grow toward maturity and life beyond the orphanage. As the church seeks to find and implement answers to the question of how to minister to institutionalized children, at least two key fronts must be addressed: the church's role in institutional orphan ministry and the church's ministry to existing orphan-care institutions.

THE CHURCH'S ROLE IN INSTITUTIONAL ORPHAN MINISTRY

*I*f we know orphaned children exist in the world, who will not be adopted or placed into healthy foster care, and we believe that the typical institutional environment of an orphanage is detrimental to the children who grow up in them, then we must be involved in acting to change institutions. We must not merely be involved in changing the trappings of the institution. We need to be agents of the Most High God who act to influence change in the DNA of the institutions. Perhaps we can best do this by starting and supporting institutions that begin with a mission to see the culture and priorities of institutional life to reflect Christ.

In America, denominations and parachurch ministries have begun a sizable number of such ministries to stand in the gap for an overwhelmed foster-care system. The problem is that the gap is wide and not nearly enough of these institutions exist. A ministry that our church has partnered with is Homes of Hope for Children in Purvis, Mississippi. This ministry is a new private work that is being built to address the urgent needs of children in our own area. Homes of Hope for Children's founder and executive director Dr. Michael Garrett is himself a graduate of the Louisiana Baptist Homes for Children and a passionate advocate for the fatherless. Homes of Hope for Children is a children's home type of ministry that seeks to provide a loving and stable home for fatherless children. Children live in small intergenerational house groups with a set of Christian houseparents. The houseparents are the frontline in caring for and discipling

> Children live in small inter-generational house groups with a set of Christian houseparents.

the children. In addition to providing a healthy home for these kids, their ministry involves three specific types of help: helping them deal with life trauma through the services of an on-site counselor; helping them catch up and achieve academically through a tutoring program; and helping them move on into adulthood through transitional assistance.

The ministry of Homes of Hope for Children is one that almost no church could afford to take on by itself. To begin and sustain ministries of this type, churches and individual believers must partner together and pool resources to succeed. Together through the work of local associations and state and national denominational conventions, we can and must pull together to begin more work like that of Homes of Hope for Children.

The church's role in international orphan care must also be examined. Perhaps we can learn something from the children's home approach in the United States can inform our approach to beginning and maintaining international institutions. Much of the orphan care that we have encountered around the world is based on the orphanage model. Large numbers of children are housed in a single building or complex. These children live in age-segregated groups in barracks-style accommodations. Shifts of workers rotate in and out to care for the children in much the same fashion as line workers in a factory. Sadly, workers, particularly in government-run institutions, see their jobs as little more than being overseers at the "child factory." They see to the children's basic needs but have little opportunity or inclination to form real attachments with the children. Seemingly, the primary considerations of the orphanage are efficiency and order, not bonding and nurture. To be sure, many Christian orphanages are better than this gross over-generalization, but sadly, many are not. Children deserve better than an impersonal institution. God deserves better than for us to create impersonal institutions. God instituted the family, and we must work to mirror the family as closely as we can in both form and function if we are to do the best for fatherless children who do not have a family.

What could happen if associations of churches made it their business to

> Sadly, workers, particularly in government-run institutions, see their jobs as little more than being overseers at the "child factory."

pool resources and begin children's homes around the globe? How could the world's orphans be impacted, and how could adding this element to our cooperation refocus local missions work? This strategy seems to hold great promise in nations in which private orphan care by religious groups is common and lawful, and it could bring revival to our local church cooperation. Caring for orphans gives us a viable reason to come together and cooperate. Our churches can accomplish together what few can accomplish alone.

The children's home model for institutional child care is a proven ministry form that has been widely adopted by Christian churches, denominations, and parachurch organizations across America for a reason. It works. In this form of orphan care, several children are placed into individual groups under the care of a set of houseparents. The children's home is comprised of a compound of several houses collected together for administrative purposes, but each individual house functions fairly independently under the authority of the children's home.

The focus is on a providing a stable "family" for each child. The children's home is the official entity that receives custody for the children from the government. Houseparents work for the children's home as employees whose duty it is to care for the children under common guidelines and policies that ensure the children's safety and provide for their nurture in Christ. The children's home can ensure that children are protected and educated. Houseparents can ensure that children are cared for and loved in a family-like setting that teaches them about Jesus, and the children can grow to maturity in a setting that approximates a God-centered family where they can be shown and taught the gospel.

Very little reason exists that American churches and denominations cannot perpetuate this ministry plan. The fact is that we possess the resources to ease the suffering of countless children by giving them a stable home and guaranteed source of support, nurture, and hope for the future. One reason cited by our own denomination for not being involved in a strategy for orphan ministry is the need to focus on planting churches and evangelization as the preeminent global mission strategy. Our contention is that mercy ministry is not a strategy apart from church planting, and is a strategy to enhance church planting.

At Temple, we have two strategic global missions foci: church planting and orphan ministry. We are committed to planting reproducible churches throughout the world. Since adopting these missional priorities, we have noticed an interesting phenomenon related to orphan ministry. A direct connection seems to be present in a number of situations we are engaged in between mercy ministry (particularly orphan ministry) and church planting. In fact, it is not an exaggeration to say that ministry effort to care for orphans has led to the planting of a number of churches. Frankly, I do not think that we should be surprised. When the church carries the heart and mission of Christ into a community and lives them out by caring the defenseless and the "least of these," the gospel is made more attractive.

For example, we have formed a partnership with an orphanage and church planting effort in Sumatra. This orphanage is home to 15 children and 2 sets of houseparents. Prior to our partnership, the orphanage workers struggled to provide for the necessities of life for the children in their care. Our support of this orphanage is different than any other partnership we have in that we only provide financial and prayer support. A church planting partner who works with them as a part of its missional vision brought this orphanage to us. The children are unadoptable, and the houseparents have become the family for these children. For only $12,000 per year, our church has been able to provide food, clothing, and education to these children to ease their suffering and supplement the love and Christian nurture they receive from their caregivers. The support of this children's home has given a living illustration of the gospel to be used by the church planting missionaries and has increased their credibility in the eyes of the community where they are planting.

Another possibility is to organize a short-term missions trip for orphan ministry. Of all the missions trip ideas that I have encountered, I think my favorite comes from HopeHouse International, a Franklin, Tennessee, ministry whose primary focus is seeing Ukrainian children adopted by Ukrainian Christian families. Each summer, HopeHouse organizes a missions cruise to Ukraine. You read that right, a missions cruise! They take up to 50 Christians for a cruise along Ukraine's Dnipro River. Instead of the normal sightseeing and recreational stops, HopeHouse teams visit orphanages. In fact, they visit ten orphanages over the course of their trip. Along the way, trip participants put on programs that share the gospel with the orphanage residents, give out Bibles and discipleship material, give away humanitarian aid, and bring the loving touch of Christ to over 1,000 children each summer. That is what I call a working vacation! HopeHouse has devised a wonderfully creative idea to take the fear out of international missions and ministering to orphans by combining a cruise with orphan ministry, and I am sure we all can as well.

Finally, the church can use her influence to elevate the public policy discussion for the fatherless. Throughout recent history, the evangelical church has shown the ability to be a political juggernaut. Why has the church borne such little fruit in changing public policy regarding the plight of the fatherless? Teaching and training regarding orphan ministry is not just something that we do other places. We must train our people to be able to respond as well. This training can be accomplished by focusing on the fatherless through the church's existing missions education programs.

The plight of the world's 200-plus million orphans is out an "out of sight, out of mind" issue for many Christians, and not something we think about as we engage politically. Collectively, evangelical Christians are a large force with the potential to influence government policy and activity on behalf of orphans worldwide. To accomplish this, we must be willing both to learn and act. We must take the time to research so as to learn what government actions hold the promise of having a positive impact on orphans' lives, and we must commit to being active in petitioning elected officials with regard to these actions.

One recent example of this type of public policy involvement is the decision by the United States to relax immigration restrictions for people living with HIV. This immigration policy change has already had a direct impact on American families adopting international orphans with HIV. The change in this government policy was due in no small part to the lobbying actions of Christians who sought to relieve a roadblock to adoption for many families. While I believe that Scripture teaches that orphan care is the responsibility of the church and not the state, we have to be involved in the affairs of the state that relate to orphans. Part of caring for orphans in their affliction is being an advocate and giving them a voice in places where they are voiceless including places of government.

THE CHURCH'S ROLE IN MINISTERING TO INSTITUTIONS

*A*s Americans, we are rich. In fact, the poorest among us are wealthy by global standards. According to the World Bank, just under 80 percent of the world's population live on less than $10 per day! Lots of us spent more than that on a meal today. This observation is not intended to stir up guilt but to acknowledge responsibility. God has blessed us in abundance, and Jesus commands us in the Gospels to be generous, sacrificial, and cheerful givers. Could it be that we have been given the wealth that God entrusts to us as a means for living out mercy ministry like we find in James 1:27?

Is it possible that one of God's important on-the-job life lessons for us is to learn about Him through the stewarding of our income and possessions on behalf of the defenseless? Of course it is. God is the ultimate giver, and He is made known and glorified in our giving. As we give sacrificially and strategically to the needs of orphans, we are giving evidence to the gospel, and we are even giving an example to our children of God and His character.

Here is an example of how we can live sacrificially and involve our children in orphan ministry. A need that surfaced in working with orphanages in Ukraine was for good quality shoes and clothing for the children. One orphanage director that we have worked with showed us that she receives a budget of less than $10 per child to clothe the children in her care. To make matters worse, the clothing that is available for her to purchase is poorly made and does not last. A ministry idea that sprang up in our church as a result of understanding this need is called Beautiful Feet. The thing that really excites me about Beautiful Feet is that it was conceived as a way to help preschoolers become involved in missions and orphan care. A group of concerned ladies who work in our preschool choir program began researching how they could make a difference for orphans and found the need for shoes was great both in our own community and in some Ukrainian orphanages.

Through connecting on the Internet to other churches and ministries who had a similar heart for orphans, these ladies found a way to have a global impact with shoes. To transport the shoes intended for Ukraine, they found a ministry who was willing to provide shipping assistance by taking extra luggage as part of their summer missions trip to several Ukrainian orphanages. Beautiful Feet is a simple project that was born out of a simple concern to meet the most basic physical needs of some orphans, and it worked. Through an annual drive, these shoes carry love and the gospel to children in need.

Another way that the church can make a difference in orphanages is by providing training and care for the orphanage staffs. As stated earlier, one of the real challenges in institutionalized care is the pattern of care adopted by many orphanages. Children in many orphanages are not neglected in the sense that their need for food, clothing, and shelter are unmet. In fact, quite the contrary is true. These children have better than a survivable situation when it comes to the physical necessities of life. What they often lack is care for the emotional necessities of life. Food, clothing, shelter, and medical care are not enough to support the well-adjusted development of an orphaned child. What they need is love and security.

In countless institutions, orphaned children have no consistency in caretakers, no one to answer their cries, and no one to attach to as a dependable source of security. To make matters worse, orphanage workers and the system they function in seems to promote emotional distance between workers and children. It seems as if the workers believe that since the children are alone in the world, it is better for them to learn how to live without becoming attached to anyone.

Food, clothing, shelter, and medical care are not enough.

A basic study of human development helps us understand that God did not fashion us to grow up this way. We don't develop in a healthy way without attaching to someone as a primary caregiver. In fact, it is not too strong to say that failure to meet the God-placed need to have a caring adult respond to a child's emotional needs and to interact with a child on a consistent basis will result in severe emotional and intellectual consequences. These consequences can also be spiritual. Failure to be nurtured by a consistent primary caregiver can also be a direct impediment to a child's ability to trust Christ later in life. Children who do not form attachment bonds early in life can grow up unable to relax and trust the world around them. Instead, they are perpetually concerned with self-preservation. They live without truly trusting anyone because they never learned how to trust. For one who has never learned to trust, the act of total surrender to God is a struggle at best and nearly impossible at worst. In the most extreme cases, children who never attach can grow to be sociopaths who live without conscience or remorse.

We can easily see the need to raise healthy, responsible adults is important, but there is a lot more at stake. In reality, changing the culture and practices of caregiving in many orphanages is not simply a humanitarian issue. It is a gospel issue. When we work to change the environment to provide attachment and security to a child as he or she grows up, we are helping those children to feel Christlike love. Feeling this love sets the stage for them to be capable of responding to Jesus.

Thankfully, we have a choice to be active in changing the philosophies and practices of the orphanages themselves. Many people are already active in these efforts. An example of a secular program designed to effect this change is the Big Sister Orphanage Program. Maryna Vashchenko, a doctoral student in the Tufts University Eliot-Pearson Department of Child Development, began the Big Sister Orphanage Program to work in orphanages in Mykolayiv, Ukraine. Her program trains students from nearby Mykolayiv University to act as caregivers for an orphaned child by visiting them five days a week and playing and talking with them. These students also help the children prepare for separation in a healthy way through talking, playing, and modeling constructive emotional behavior. Vashchenko and her advisors at Tufts University have great hopes that her program will make a difference in the orphanage culture of Ukraine. In an interview for the *Tufts Journal*, one of her advisors said, "I am confident that her work will have an impact on the quality of care and the goodness of policies and practices in a deteriorating and tragic system so clearly in need of reform."

Vashchenko has identified a problem and sought to meet the need, but our goal is for a greater end. How much more should we who are joined to Christ be motivated to meet this need and to love them like Jesus? Imagine what would happen if the church mobilized missionaries to go and love orphaned children in their orphanages as a tangible expression of Jesus' love? What if we sent college students as summer missionaries to minister to orphanage workers and the children in their care? What if these students were prepared to share the gospel with them and to show them how to live the gospel out, by caring for orphaned children in a way that models the love, redemption, restoration, and security that can be found in Christ? I think it could make a kingdom-sized difference.

This is a relatively new idea in Christian orphan care and one that needs to be explored by the church as a viable avenue for mercy ministry and gospel proclamation.

LIFESONG FOR ORPHANS

One example of a ministry that is taking significant strides to "bring joy and purpose to orphans" is Lifesong for Orphans. Through its Constant Christian Presence (CCP) program, Lifesong for Orphans gives churches the opportunity to adopt an orphanage and provide nurturing Christian care for its children. The goal of the CCP program is for a Christian mentor to develop loving, trusting relationships with an orphanage's children and staff to help them develop and mature into followers of Jesus.

An orphanage adoption by a church provides for a national believer to serve as a CCP mentor to an orphanage as a full-time minister to the children living there. The mentor builds relationships with the orphaned children, cares for them spiritually and emotionally, and teaches them biblical principles, Christian character, job skills, relationships skills, and more. Lifesong also coordinates improving the living conditions of the orphaned children through administrating financial support and coordinating missions teams who come to work in the orphanage. They also provide transitional assistance for children who age-out of the orphanage system through a transition home. Currently, Lifesong ministers to approximately 1,000 orphans in eastern Ukraine through its CCP program. According to Andy Lehman, vice-president of Lifesong for Orphans:

We believe firmly that the only way we can change kids' lives eternally is by engaging the US church and the local Ukrainian church to come alongside the needs of orphan children. Lifesong invites US churches to consider making a two- to three-year commitment to "adopt" one specific orphanage/facility. This Adopt-an-Orphanage commitment can include:

Yearly Missions Trip— The church sends a team of up to 12—15 people to visit a Ukrainian orphanage/facility in which Lifesong does significant orphan care work on a continuing basis. This is a prime opportunity for the US Christians to work alongside of and encourage the Ukrainian Christians . . . as you both serve orphans! These trips usually have a daily Vacation Bible School–like component as well as some minor construction opportunities.

Financially Support CCP Ministry—Regular financial contributions are needed to support ongoing CCP work. Churches and individuals can help financially support the indigenous "Constant Christian Presence" program and mentors (Ukrainian staff) that will do the year-round, daily mentoring and discipleship.

Our prayer is that churches in significant numbers will begin to include providing missions workers to orphanages in their mission strategies. In the process of learning about orphanages and the children that grow up in them, we are constantly learning more about how we can make a difference for Christ, and you can too. Ministry does not have to be grand to be good. God has blessed each of us and each of our churches with sufficient resources to make a difference in the lives of some institutionalized children. Our task is to identify our resources and the opportunities that God has placed before us and to bring them together each day!

— RM

Two Orphan Stories— Dima and Vanya

The value of Lifesong's CCP program can be seen in the lives of Dima and Vanya:

*D*ima never knew his father. He lived with his mother in Kharkov, Ukraine, who took care of him until he was six years old. Around that time she turned to drinking, quit her job, and left Dima to take care of himself.

In order to earn some money and care for himself, Dima would collect glass bottles or take the garbage out for his neighbors. Unable to live off of what little money he made, he often rummaged through the garbage for food. Sometimes his neighbors would feed him, but in time they decided to call the authorities and let them deal with the situation. In 1997, nine-year-old Dima was taken to a homeless shelter for three months and then sent to Loubetin Orphanage. Once there, Dima never saw his mother again. She died of alcohol abuse in 2007.

Six years later, Lifesong introduced their CCP program to Loubetin Orphanage. Dima noticed something different about these staff members and volunteers from the local community. These people were kind, even to orphans like him. They played games with him and developed relationships with him and his friends. They didn't treat him like an outcast, as most in their culture did, but encouraged him and loved him as he was. Most importantly, these people introduced Dima to Jesus Christ, engaged him in Bible study and reading, and provided Christian counseling and mentorship.

Through the CCP program Dima was able to develop true meaningful relationships, get involved in a local church, and participate in summer camps and after school programs where he could have fun with other kids and learn more about the love of Christ. In 2005, Dima began attending a local church regularly and accepted Jesus as his personal Lord and Savior. He was baptized the following year.

Now Dima is a resident at one of Lifesong's Transition Homes in Kharkov, a home designed to help those aging out of the orphanage system to transition into productive independent lifestyles. Through this program he has learned the value of self-discipline, both spiritually and physically. He is able to cook and clean for himself, has attended a culinary program at a local college, and works part-time at a top-rated restaurant in Kharkov, where his boss describes him as being hardworking and responsible. In church he is involved in youth ministry and even preaches from time to time!

> Through this program he has learned the value of self-discipline, both spiritually and physically.

While Dima has changed greatly since he was that little boy on the street, he never forgot the hardships he went through. He dreams of someday owning his own restaurant, where he can provide an entrance for those who are poor and hungry.

Vanya was abandoned at birth, and spent the first 11 years of his life in 4 different orphanages. In 2002, when he was 11 years old, Vanya moved to Sachnovsheena Orphanage, where he encountered new difficulties. Being dark-skinned, Vanya was discriminated against not only by his culture, but also by the other children.

Two years later, when Lifesong started their CCP program in Sachnovsheena, Vanya describes the staff visits as "something bright, once in a while." They provided him with a safe place to go; with friendship and mentorship; things Vanya had not found anywhere else.

To these staff members and volunteers, one thing was evident. Vanya was smart. He had a hunger for knowledge and an amazing talent for learning English. This was something director, Denis Poshelok noticed almost instantly. He soon got Vanya involved in English lessons and under this tutelage, Vanya flourished.

Vanya also developed a strong connection with Lifesong staff member, Dima, who helped him learn through Bible study and discussion. Referring to Dima as his "spiritual father," Vanya remembers being listened to and challenged in those discussions. And though he resisted the gospel at first, through relationships like this, loving examples from others on the Lifesong team and educational support he began to see Christ's love in action. It did not take long before Vanya knew that he wanted a relationship of his own with Jesus.

Now at 19, Vanya rises above standards and expectations. He lives in one of Lifesong's Transition Homes, studies English at the local college, translates for Americans who come to visit, and mentors younger boys at the orphanage in the same way the Lifesong staff once mentored him.

Once a family brings a child home, the church has a whole host of opportunities for ministry.

6

HOW DO YOU DO ADOPTION SUPPORT AND FUNDING?

*B*eing one of the pastors in a church that is vocal about orphan care and adoption, it seems like a week never goes by without talking to someone who is considering adoption. Adoptions are becoming common around us, and as more families adopt, more families seem to be considering adoption as a means of living out the gospel. To illustrate, I want to relate a funny conversation that I had with a good friend about adoption. One day we were talking, and he mentioned that he and his wife were praying about adopting. *Great*, I thought, *another family that God is dealing with about caring for the fatherless!* So, I got ready to have the "standard" adoption conversation. You see, when I am asked about adoption, people typically ask about how Denise and I knew God was leading us to adopt. Or they want to know things about the process like how much it costs or how long it takes to adopt. Well, let's just say that my friend's concern was far from the norm.

He said, "Here is my struggle. I don't want to adopt because everyone else is doing it. I have been guilty in the past of jumping into hobbies and things just because lots of other people loved them and were so passionate about them. I got excited and then lost interest. I don't want to be 'that guy' with adoption. It's too important, and I want to do it for the right reasons."

Wow! What an honest statement. I was refreshed by his candor. It also got me to thinking about what is the "right" reason to adopt. Recently, I heard a sermon by John Piper at the Christian Alliance for Orphans Summit VI. In that sermon, Piper said, "All adoption and all orphan care by Christians—by those who are justified by grace alone through faith alone on the basis of Christ alone—is done by *faith*." Like everything else we do in life after we come to Jesus in surrender and repentance, adoption is an act of faith. The "right" answer is that we adopt as an outworking of our faith, no more and no less.

Adoption is God's will. It says so throughout the New Testament, and boy, should we be glad! That's how we were brought into the kingdom and made heirs of the Most High. Our task in the church is to walk with people as they wrestle with God's will and how it intersects with their lives. Maybe the question that we should be giving families an opportunity to wrestle with is: *Why shouldn't I adopt?* If we know that adoption is God's revealed will, and adoption is His plan A for both bringing us into the kingdom and caring for orphans, then why shouldn't we assume that adoption is God's will for all Christian families and then look for signs that God isn't leading us to adopt!?

> As a family of faith, the church can help families through pre-adoption guidance and support.

So, as we challenge families to consider adoption through our preaching and teaching, we have to provide them with resources to inform them and sustain them on their journey. As a family of faith, the church can help families through pre-adoption guidance and support. To stir up people about adoption without providing discipling opportunities to help them explore and grow in obedience regarding adoption is unreasonable. As a church, we have found a great partner to help us include adoption-related issues into our plan for discipling. We have partnered with a ministry called Adoption Discovery (www.adoptiondiscovery.org) to host small groups to help people explore adoption as an outworking of their faith.

Adoption Discovery provides leadership training for people in your church to be qualified to guide prospective adoptive parents through a seven-week small group so they will better understand the process and be able to make informed choices about adoption. Adoption Discovery prepares leaders to lead their group to understand all the adoption options available to them, to discover and work through family questions and expectations as they relate to the adoption of a child, and to foster a community of support for families as they move forward in adopting.

What we have seen through the Adoption Discovery process is that families are given all the information that they need to pray and work through the question of whether to adopt, and they are introduced to a larger community of support through these groups and their leaders. Whether or not you partner with an organization like Adoption Discovery, any church that teaches the doctrine of adoption and promotes adoption should include some sort of functional small-group experience for people to be able to learn more about adoption and to consider how best to apply the truth of God's Word as followers of Jesus.

As we have alluded to earlier, adoption (particularly international adoption) can be costly, but there are also many, many ways to afford to adopt.

A quick search of the Internet will uncover some really creative families putting an entrepreneurial spirit to work on behalf of bringing orphaned children home to their families; by selling everything from self-produced albums to coffee to T-shirts. Even current US tax laws provide some help by offering for a substantial tax credit ($13,170 in 2010) to help defray some of the expenses. The problem with the tax credit is cash flow since it can only be claimed after the adoption is finalized. The good news is that the church can minister in this area by helping to relieve financial barriers to adoption.

One way that our church has sought to help is by beginning a ministry fund called the Abba Father Ministry. The Abba Father Fund gives an outlet for individuals and families within the church, who are not adopting, to meet the financial needs of those who are. The Abba Father Fund plan is simple: Adopting families agree to a no-interest covenant promise to pay back an adoption grant. Adoption grants are made on the basis of need only after families have a qualified home study and are ready to adopt. Repayment is only planned to begin after at least a year after the adoption is finalized to allow the family to get adjusted financially.

In the first two-and-a-half years of ministry, the Abba Father Ministry collected more than $75,000 and helped more than a dozen orphans find forever families—with more on the way. At Temple, we are thankful to have the resources to have a ministry like this that can be sustained here, and for ladies like Jill Hodge and Sandy Mayfield, who felt God's leadership to begin it.

What if you are in a church that would like to partner with other churches to pool together to help others afford to adopt? Let us suggest a few excellent resource partners. First, Abba Fund (www.abbafund.org) and Lifesong for Orphans (www.lifesongfororphans.org)

They are both parachurch ministries that help your church establish and manage an adoption fund. These ministries are excellent places to invest resources to be loaned on a no-interest basis to Christian families who are adopting as they manage a self-perpetuating fund dedicated to liberating as many fatherless children as possible into loving Christian homes.

At our church, we are blessed to have a great number of people with the skill and calling to manage the Abba Father fund. It is a best-fit scenario for us to keep our fund in-house. In talking with my friend, Andy Leman at Lifesong for Orphans, he articulated some of the barriers that a church might face as it considers whether to manage a fund or establish a fund and have it managed by a ministry like Abba Fund of Lifesong? Here are Andy's thoughts:

Abba Fund and Lifesong both help provide solutions to the top three most common barriers to churches creating adoption funds.

1. Barrier: The church staff has a "plate that is already full" and to administer an adoption fund would add one more ministry responsibility to an already busy pastoral staff

Solution: Abba Fund or Lifesong will manage/facilitate the fund and carry the administrative load on behalf of church, using mutually agreed upon criteria (reviewing applications, accounting, donor receipts, disbursing funds on behalf of adoption, etc.).

2. Barrier: The church feels uncomfortable/awkward approving/denying its own families (viewing financials, etc.).

Solution: Abba Fund or Lifesong will provide all the screening, reviewing, approving/denying as a "partner" on behalf of the church, using mutually agreed upon criteria for those decisions.

3. Barrier: The operation of an adoption fund is unfamiliar territory for a church.

Solution: Abba Fund or Lifesong has passion and expertise in adoption funding processes to maximize stewardship. They use established grant/loan procedures and maintain IRS and ECFA standards that ensure financial integrity and keep the church from "reinventing the wheel."

And one of the best aspects . . . Abba Fund or Lifesong manages and administers the Adoption Fund—at no cost to churches!

Andy shared a great success story with me of a local church that began a modest adoption fund but, with God's blessing and good planning, has seen incredible growth. Tapestry, the Adoption/Foster Care Ministry of Irving Bible Church (http://tapestry.irvingbible.org/index.php?id=1580) began their adoption funding ministry with Lifesong with an initial investment of only $10,000. With prayer, hard work, and faithfulness, they have maximized stewardship well by utilizing both interest-free loans and adoption matching grants so effectively that they have helped 14 children be adopted and have mobilized over $115,000! They did this by using matching grants as a catalyst in helping families raise money needed for adoption and through accumulation of interest-free loan repayments. What a great example of faithfulness and entrepreneurial creativity in the body of Christ! I pray that we may follow their lead in discovering new and inventive ways to maximize our resources to spread the gospel and give fathers to the fatherless.

Another good partner organization is the Southern Baptist Convention's Adoption Fund for Ministers. At the 2010 Southern Baptist Convention Pastor's Conference, conference president Kevin Ezell announced the creation of a fund to help Southern Baptist pastors and missionaries afford the cost of adoption. An initial offering was received in the amount of $26,000 and a goal of an endowment of $1.5 million has been established to see the work of adoption be carried on for many generations through the families of Southern Baptist pastors and missionaries.

The church also can minister by helping families find adoption resources and partners to assist them along the adoption journey. Think of it like the church as a clearinghouse of information for Christian families as they move along the decision process toward adoption. We are merely trying to give them as many good options as possible as our connections grow through the ever-expanding missional global adoption community.

Throughout the Christian community there are a host of reputable organizations and agencies that are dedicated to providing a variety of ministry services to assist the church in adoption ministry. For instance, our church partners with a number of Christian adoption providers to offer information and support seminars throughout the year. While we are very careful to use due diligence to do careful screening of any one organization that we would host for a seminar or allow to use our facilities for a meeting,

We are very careful not to get into the business of recommending agencies, and we would recommend that strategy to you. Spread the opportunities. Make new friends. Certainly, there will be people and organizations that you will develop comfortable relationships with over time, and that you will come back to time and time again to work with cooperatively, but by venturing out to host new organizations for adoption and orphan ministry emphases, your church can continue to encourage a continued focus.

> I have just motivated some first-time dad to want to punch me in the neck!

We need to structure our churches to provide support and encouragement through the paperwork and waiting of the adoption process. Frankly, my wife and I have not had our family the "conventional" way, so I am not expert on conventional families, but from the outside looking in, it looks mostly predictable. (It feels like I should insert one of those little smiley face things here because I am sure I have just motivated some first-time dad to want to punch me in the neck!). OK, so no birth process or path to parenting is ever predictable, but all things being equal, if you find out you are expecting a child the conventional way, you generally expect that you will bring a child home from the hospital 32–36 weeks later, right? Not always, but anything that doesn't fit that pattern is an exception. Adoption is different.

In adoption, anything that fits a pattern is different. There are so many different paths. There are all kinds of paths that fit different family types, different countries, and at some point you come to realize that every adoption really doesn't fit a pattern at all. It's a roller-coaster ride.

You begin the process with a home study. A home study is a flurry of paperwork and interviews. Quite frankly, it's a little scary. At least it was for us. It doesn't have to be. Your social worker has a job to do. He or she is entrusted by an agency and licensed by the state to make sure that you have a stable, healthy home according to the laws of your state to accommodate the number of children you are seeking to adopt. This assessment includes emotional, physical, and financial stability. They are helping you make an assessment of your reasons for adoption and your plan for adoption and the adjustment to come.

Most states require that your social worker make several post-placement visits and reports before your adoption is final. This is not because Big Brother is watching! They are closing the loop on helping in your adjustment to becoming a family. This is why it is crucial to choose a social worker that you are comfortable with and who shares your worldview. They are part of your team! Denise and I are so thankful for the three wonderful, godly ladies that the Father has brought onto our team in the last seven years. They are part of our story. They are family. Not just because they have helped us get our kids but also because they are our sisters. There were many, many tough days along the way when we were struggling to find meaning in the process that they just understood because they were our sisters. We share a Father, and that is vital.

The roller coaster isn't limited to home studies and social workers and soon it gives way to waiting, and the waiting can be agony. It can be that you are waiting for a birth mother to select your family from among a number of other profiles to be the one to become her baby's forever family, or it can be that you are waiting for a government's approval to travel to adopt. Often the waiting can seem like a series of encouraging false starts only to seem like you are back at square one. We all need a network of support as we endure the ups and downs that are sure to come as we wait through the uncertainty of the process. One of the great things that I have seen God do in our church, Temple, is to grow that type of community of support.

Literally dozens of families that are at all phases in the journey have banded together for prayer, meals, talks, sharing information, sharing resources, babysitting, helping each other pack for an international adoption trip on three days' notice (yes, it's happened more than once!). You name it. We've probably done it. In the process, I think we have all learned a lot about true biblical community, and that community isn't just limited to "adopting" families.

There are many other people who have joined us. They are not adopting themselves, but they love adoption and they love us and they want to be on the team. We have a lot to learn. Over time, we have discovered ministries in other churches that are much more organized than ours. Ours is much more organic. We get together by word of mouth. We meet needs because we make needs known, and we pray and work together. We just kind of do it. I know other churches that function in their foster and adoption ministries with organization precision, and I envy them. We're just not there. As a church, our core values are to be biblical, relational, missional, and global. In this area, we are highly relational. Often, the greatest gift that we can give each other is the gift of Christian community.

Remember the friend that I began this chapter by talking about? As I am writing this sentence, he and his family are in China completing the adoption of their daughter. It's a great story. I hope you can hear it someday! A few days before his family left, he came by my office. It was a great visit. We've really become close friends in the last several years, but we are different in many ways. My friend is an outdoorsman intellectual, while I think camping is not having cable television. We have a lot of fun talking theology while he tries to educate me on the finer points of field dressing wild game. The truth is I am pretty sure he could live off the land with nothing but his wits and a Buck knife; if there is a natural disaster in the area, I want him on my team! I am convinced he would have worn camouflage to his wedding if his wife had allowed. You get the picture.

> So my friend and I prayed and we laughed and we cried!

Before he left, he came by to talk and told me that he was scared. I laughed. You see, I'm scared too. We each adopted a son with some pretty deep emotional scars and some pretty devastating hurts in his past. Who wouldn't be scared; but we serve the God who created and who heals! So my friend and I prayed and we laughed and we cried! It was a big nasty cry. It was a good cry. It was the kind of cry that you can only have with someone you love and who loves you deeply. In adopting, you need that. You need lots of that, and the church must be that sort of community.

Once a family brings a child home, the church has a whole host of opportunities for ministry. One great way that we the church can help is to step in and take the burden off the family members so that they can focus on bonding with their new addition(s). As explained in this book's stories, bonding and attachment to parents are so crucial for healthy adjustment, growth, development, and even spiritual growth that the initial days of a child coming home need to be an intense time for parents to focus on the child, or children, and their needs.

The church can mobilize to feed, shop for, do laundry for, clean house for, and in general ease the daily pressure for an adoptive family. It is a huge help. We understand the need for this in the early days for birth families, but the need for new adoptive families may be even more crucial. In birth families, biology is on their side. Babies' brains are at a stage at which they are ready to bond. If the child being adopting is not an infant, the task is more difficult to do and the need to focus on bonding is more crucial. The church can make a huge difference in giving a family that opportunity.

The church can also become a great source of reference for adoptive families. Perhaps one the most valuable things I learned in seminary was through a counseling class. In that class, the professor took great pains to convince us that as pastors most of us were ill-equipped to counsel most anyone about most anything beyond offering them biblical guidance. We didn't have enough training or clinical practice to do real counseling. Of course he was right. His answer was simple. He contended that we would most always be one of the first sources of counsel for many people, but that as pastors we must develop the skill of referral. Pastors have a responsibility to know the competent and credible counseling resources in their communities to be able to refer people on to see. I have learned while being in a church that is experiencing many adoptions that quite the same idea is necessary. And I have seen the New Testament concept about the nature of the body of Christ confirmed along the way. God has truly gifted and resourced the body for every good work. Time and time again, we have seen the network of relationships present within the church and extending from the church come to bear many times at just the right time for an adoptive family with needs.

Adoptive families may need doctors, lawyers, therapists, social workers, and a host of others to assist them along the way on their journey. You will be surprised how many of these people are already in your church or already known to people in your church. Don't be afraid to call them and enlist their help. Collect their information together in one place and give this information to new adoptive families as a part of new/prospective adoptive families resource pack. Collecting these things together can save many hours and much stress on a new family trying to sort out the way to get started out right.

Adoption is a big step for a family. For a church, care for the family can take the shape of both very big and very small things that make a world of difference. Everyone in the church can do something to participate and support adoptive families. With a little of your time, talent, treasure, your love, or all four of these gifts, you can make a significant contribution in the life of a family who is making all the difference in the life of a child!

— RM

An Adoption Story—Adam and Jill Hodge

My wife and I decided to adopt two older children from Uganda two years ago. There were many reasons that contributed to our decision to adopt as well as our decision to choose the African continent. Our primary reason for the adoption was born out of our understanding that we too have been adopted by God through Christ Jesus according to Ephesians 1:5. Inevitably, when people hear that we have adopted from Africa, they marvel at the "blessing" that the African children have received and inquire about the significant change that must have occurred in their lives at the time of the adoption. While it is true that there have been significant changes in the children's lives, there have been great changes in the life of both my wife and me as well.

Practically, for starters, the volume in our home has increased exponentially by adding two children to our existing quiver of two. If you've never experienced the joy of a dance party with four children under the age of ten, your eardrums are missing out. In addition, our bedtime routine has been extended to approximately two hours. Baths, bed, kisses, hugs, tucks, stories, water, more kisses and hugs, pee-pee, poo-poo, kisses and hugs, and finally, lights out. Then, another drink. I won't even mention the grocery bill, water bill, clothing budget, doctors visits, and so many more little surprises.

While the practical aspects of adoption have been significant, the spiritual aspects have both challenged and taught us the most. We are being humbled and sanctified daily as we depend on Christ to give us what it takes to make this adoption thing work. We have successes and failures. It has allowed us to participate in the sufferings of Christ. I think that too few people talk about the pain and difficulty associated with adopting. It is not an easy path to walk as many who have adopted will attest. However, was it an easy path that Christ walked while on this earth? Was it easy for Him to live among sinners in a sin-soaked world away from the perfection that He had known? Was it easy for Him to be despised and rejected by men? After all, He was a man acquainted with sorrow and grief. Was it easy for Christ to be beaten nearly to death and then hung on the Cross until dead? That is what it took for God to adopt me into His family. Why then should I expect to escape suffering when practicing the mandate that I should look after orphans?

What has adoption done in our lives? It has allowed us to grow closer to the heart of God as we imitate our Father in the sufferings of adoption. As we attempt to live in obedience to His Word and as imitators of God, we receive blessings that only He can deliver. He teaches us that He is our Abba and we are His children. He holds us and loves us as a true and perfect Father. I thank Him for allowing me and my wife the privilege of following Him in the beauty that is adoption.

— AHJ

If we are to live out the call of James 1:27 in America, then we must begin to rethink how our churches engage foster-care ministry.

7

HOW CAN THE CHURCH RESPOND IN FOSTER CARE?

*A*s we consider the plight of the fatherless and our response, we have to be careful not to forget those children who are closest to us. According to recent statistics, there are just fewer than 500,000 children who reside in American foster care each year. A whole host of reasons exist for why children may find themselves in foster care. Many are the victims of abuse, neglect, and abandonment. Others are placed in temporary care as a result of the illness or temporary disability of a parent or primary caregiver. No matter the reason that a child finds himself in foster care, almost certainly fear, uncertainty, and trauma are part of the journey.

For the purposes of our discussion in this book, foster care is simply the process by which a minor who has been made a ward of the state is placed in the private or group care home of a state-certified caregiver referred to as a foster parent. The state, through the family court and its child protective services stand *in loco parentis* (in the place of parents) for the minor, making all legal decisions while the foster parent is responsible for the day to day care of the child.

While the modern foster-care system is a function of the state and federal government, government responsibility for foster children is a relatively recent historical development. In fact, the beginnings of the modern foster-care system in American can be traced directly to the efforts of Christians concerned with the welfare of neglected and abandoned children in the burgeoning urban areas of America in the mid-1800s.

Charles Loring Brace, a pastor and the director of the New York Children's Aid Society, became concerned over the number of immigrant children sleeping on the streets of New York City. Moved with compassion, Brace conceived a plan to advertise throughout the American South and West to attract families to take these children into their homes and care for them. Certainly, Brace's plan was not perfect, and history reflects that there were children who found their way from one bad situation to another through the placing out of the orphan train movement. Despite the imperfection of Brace's plan, one fact is indisputable. Brace and his contemporaries recognized the need for the church to take responsibility for the fatherless and to care for them in their affliction. It is a bit ironic that his ministry may have also started the shift in America to move orphan care away from the church and toward the state. The actions of Charles Loring Brace and those of his co-laborers in founding this crude fostering ministry movement brought the plight of these ignored children to the notice of the state. From this effort, the modern government system of child welfare, child placing, and foster care was born.

Today, we are facing quite the opposite peril as was faced in Brace's day. The government is present and active in the lives of thousands upon thousands of abused, neglected, and abandoned children in America. Sadly, in many cases, we, the church of the Lord Jesus Christ, are the ones who are absent. As Christians, have we decided that since these children are provided for on some level by the government, they are not our problem? Certainly, not all Christians have abandoned foster care as an avenue of ministry, but for the most part, churches are not engaged in purposeful, systematic plans and activities to make a difference for Christ in the foster children of their communities. If we are to live out the call of James 1:27 in America, then we must begin to rethink how our churches engage foster-care ministry.

Ministry with foster children is in some ways similar to other orphan ministries, but in other ways it is profoundly different. As the foster-care system has grown in America, the way in which we care for the fatherless has produced an entire subculture with unique customs, practices, and vocabulary. To see how the church can be effective in living out the gospel among the foster children of our nation, I think we need to take a little time to understand some common things about the foster-care system.

Perhaps the most significant difference between ministries to foster children and other orphan ministries is that the long-term focus of the foster-care system is on reunification of the family of origin. The primary objective of everyone in the social-services system is to promote healing and restoration to a child's family so that the child may return to live a healthy, safe, and beneficial life within her family. Statistics regarding foster care in the United States reflect this priority.

In 2008, there were approximately 463,000 children living in foster care. Of those children, roughly 273,000 entered foster care in 2008 and 285,000 exited foster care with only about 123,000 of the total number of children having been placed into permanent state custody and awaiting adoption. What these numbers demonstrate is that the child-welfare system is heavily weighted toward giving parents opportunities to correct the activities and circumstances that resulted in their children being removed from their care so that the children can be reintegrated into healthy families of origin. While this is a laudable goal, we have to realize that it brings with it some significant challenges for the child.

Multiple attempts to bring healing and restoration to a troubled family may result in a series of severe disruptions to the child. In fact, many foster children find themselves bounced in and out of foster care countless times with each disruption adding to their trauma. Reuniting families is a worthy goal, but we must not discount the tremendous toll that uncertainty and severing attachments have on children and their development. Kids need stability. Compounding the trust issues that are formed by removing a child from his home, family, friends, school, and community is the endless cycle that many children face in being moved from one unfamiliar placement to another. These issues are often even further compounded by a lack of a sense of safety and security that may result in struggles such as poor academic achievement; poor emotional, social, or behavioral adjustment; or significant difficulties in forming healthy

> In fact, many foster children find themselves bounced in and out of foster care countless times.

relationships. Sadly, the impermanence and instability that children experience moving through the foster system results in a heavy toll upon many.

We must remember that despite the trauma and significant challenges that these children face, they are just like other children. We must approach our ministry to them by remembering that they are simply children whom Jesus loves and whom He would have us love. They may be varied in their age, culture, needs, and life experiences, but they are common in at least three ways.

First, they have all faced some sort of significant trauma or loss in their pasts. Second, they all yearn for a normal life characterized by permanence and hope. Third, like all of us, these children desperately want and need a safe and loving family to care for them even if for just a season while their family is changing.

In Christ, we have solutions to these needs. We are in relationship with the God of the universe who created these children valuable. God is for them. He makes provision for their healing and restoration in Christ. We are the ambassadors of Christ who have news of a hopeful future in the gospel. We bear the message of the Savior who died to provide them with ultimate safety, love, and family. In our reaching out to them in their hurts and afflictions, not only can we ease their current suffering, but we can also give evidence to Jesus' love for them.

Adding to the difficulty of foster care is the lack of resources in many states and communities. By and large, the child protective services programs provided by states are overburdened and underfunded. Typically, caseworkers find themselves overwhelmed by the number of family cases they manage. They are given insufficient resources to provide help to families of origin find healing and stability. These caseworkers also find it challenging to provide stable interim home situations for children as their families are either restored or severed. The church can have a real and immediate impact on the lives of everyone in the child-welfare system by coming alongside them and lightening their burden in appropriate ways. There are at least three broad areas that the church can address in ministering to the fatherless in foster care:

• becoming foster families,
• providing aid to foster families,
• and supporting foster care.

WAYS TO MINISTER:
ACTIONS CHURCHES CAN TAKE IN OUR COMMUNITIES

The first and most obvious way that the church can make an immediate impact to foster children is to take them in and provide them with a stable, loving, and Christ-centered environment. The body of Christ is responsible to care for the fatherless, and that care extends to the temporarily fatherless as well. Christian families are the best place for disconnected, hurting, and hopeless children to be placed. Our families are also the best place for these children to feel and see the love of God and to understand that God has a purpose and a plan for their lives. Remember, Deuteronomy 6 tells us that the role of the home is to pass on to the next generation the story of God's love, His offer of redemption, and His mission. For these children whose families are failing them in this responsibility, we must stand in the gap.

To illustrate how the church can respond to immediate needs within the foster-care system, take the example provided for us by our friend David Platt and the Church at Brook Hills in Birmingham, Alabama. In response to a recent preaching and teaching series in the Book of James, the Church at Brook Hills inquired as to how they could help child protective services in their area care for the fatherless in their own community. Actually, they asked what a miracle would look like to the child protective services workers. The answer was 100 families who would commit to become foster families. The Church at Brook Hills took up this idea and offered its members the opportunity to commit to foster care. More than 160 families answered the call! You may be struggling to imagine a church with 160 families much less an outpouring of mercy ministry of this magnitude. So, let's bring the example down to size.

What would it take for one family in your church to commit to foster care? As we have presented earlier in this book, it is the privilege and responsibility of pastors to lead churches to respond to the fatherless by teaching what God commands His children to do in caring for them. It is also the responsibility of church leaders to give practical outlets for their church people to respond to the Word in action. By leading Christians to become active in foster care in our communities, we could transform the social-services system for Christ while making an eternal difference in fatherless children. And, best of all, these actions will give the world a tangible picture of who Jesus is and will bring Him much glory!

A great way to promote foster care in our churches is to personalize these children by putting faces and names of children awaiting placement before people. While this is not always possible as a result of state privacy laws, many state and local child protective services have a Tuesday's Child type of program in which they have children's names, pictures, and even a little bit of their story for display as a recruiting tool for foster families.

Your church could offer to host such a display in a prominent area like your church foyer during a time of emphasis on orphan ministry or during high-traffic times like Christmas and Easter programs as a way to help the state recruit Christian families to foster in your community. We have found that working in partnership with the Children's and Family Services workers and our local representative Wendy's Wonderful Kids worker from the Dave Thomas Foundation for Adoption, we are able to host a display occasionally.

In addition to recruiting potential foster families, the church can also become a place of equipping and support for foster families. Something as simple as offering your church facilities to your city's child placing agency as a consistent place where they can offer training can be a great help. What if in addition to recruiting families and providing a place for them to be trained, your church took connecting and loving those families on an ongoing ministry? What might that ongoing ministry entail? We can't think too practically.

One idea is collecting and dispersing essential supplies and meals for foster families who have recently taken a placement. In many cases, a foster family who has a child placed with them may do so without much notice. Emergencies typically don't run on a schedule. What a blessing to a family who is trying to focus on the care of a new foster child to have things like diapers, formula, and toys brought to them by the church so that they do not have to leave their care for a child to see to these necessary details. This could be a really significant ministry outlet for people within the church who want to minister to the fatherless but cannot adopt or foster themselves.

Another idea we have found helpful to our local Children's and Family Services staff is hosting a picnic for foster families. The church provides a day of recreation for these families who are sacrificing themselves daily on behalf of the fatherless. As an added benefit, the picnic has become a prime recruitment tool for Children's and Family Services as they seek to get new families acquainted with fostering by meeting and spending time with those who are already fostering.

Another concern the church could address for foster children involves the inherent indignity that often is part of the process. Imagine being a child who has been swept from her home and whisked away through a series of cars, vans, and offices with little familiar to accompany them. Often little or nothing that they call theirs accompanies them, and what little they do have is crammed into garbage bags. A simple act of kindness like providing personal care items, some simple toys, and a backpack or duffel bag to hold their possessions is a great way to restore a little dignity to an older child. In seeking to rebuild a little of his dignity, we are ministering to child's affliction and recognizing him or her as a loved and valued creation of the Most High God!

Foster care can be difficult. Traumatized children who do not know how to relate to their new surroundings and often do not even have the capacity to relax from a fight-or-flight emotional state to enjoy the security and safety of their new life. Foster parents, though trained in advance to expect the difficulty, are experiencing their own issues of adjustment, and these foster parents face the stress of 24-hours-a-day, seven-day-a-week responsibility for these children under the often confusing and frightening burden of state policies and regulations. Fostering can be tough, and foster families need to have breaks to rest, relax, regroup, and seek God. We can provide them with opportunities for these breaks, but doing so is a little more complex than you might think.

> Fostering can be tough, and foster families need to have breaks to rest, relax, regroup, and seek God.

Because foster children are the responsibility of the state, a host of policies and regulations govern whom foster parents can leave to care for their foster children in their absence. You can check with local officials to determine policies that apply in your area, but typically, individuals and families can become certified to be babysitters or to provide respite care. In fact, part of the intake process for many new families becoming qualified to foster is identifying several friends and family members who can help in these areas. Babysitters are people who can be called upon to provide a few hours of relief to the parents and respite care providers are people who are prepared to take care of the foster children for several days to allow the family to get away for rest. Qualified babysitters and respite care providers must be cleared through the same background checking procedures as those used for foster parents and must receive training. By creating a pool of willing, cleared, and trained relief volunteers, the church can anticipate this need for families and can offer a short-term, flexible option for church members to become involved in ministering to the fatherless.

As mentioned earlier, many children who are placed out in foster care face significant challenges in academic performance and appropriate social relationships. They are often behind in school as a result of their past abuse and neglect. Many also have great difficulty in forming and maintaining healthy social relationships brought on by poor modeling and abuse. We can help these children by volunteering as tutors and mentors. Christian men and women of all ages and backgrounds can be used mightily by God to show the love and compassion of Christ to these children by teaching them and by showing them how to live. As we spend time with them, we have the opportunity to speak the gospel into their lives, and the gospel will make all the difference.

> Many children in foster care face significant challenges in academic performance and social relationships.

In Deuteronomy 6, God tells His people how to communicate His story to the next generation. He says we should "teach them diligently to your children, and shall talk of them when you sit in your house, and when you walk by the way, and when you lie down, and when you rise." As we get to know them, we can sprinkle our conversations with Jesus. As we help them learn math and science, we can show them the God who is the author of math and science and help them to see that He is the same God who loves and cares for them deeply. For kids who do not have a mama or a papa who will teach them about God, His plan for their life, or His provision for them in Jesus, they can never have too many significant "other" adults who will. By using the serious needs that these children have, we can come close and use the context of our relationship to earn the right to give them Jesus.

The church can also rally to foster families in prayer support. The darkness and distress that surrounds many foster children is spiritual warfare. So many of the emotional and spiritual needs these children have are severe and tangled. Often, we don't even know where to begin. Why not begin in prayer?

Organizing a prayer ministry that lifts up foster families is a great way to get more of the church involved. When a family is anticipating a placement, why not have a team prayerwalk their home and neighborhood? Why not schedule a round-the-clock prayer vigil to labor in prayer with a family who is getting started with a new child in their home? How about organizing a prayer chain of people who will pray and pass on the prayer requests that families can reach out to when the going gets tough? Making prayer a part of the design of our orphan ministries and not an afterthought acknowledges our dependence upon God for what we need to answer His call to care for orphans.

There is another significant need that the church can meet in the area of foster care. It is in interim care for children (particularly infants) awaiting adoption. I want to introduce you to Tim and Andra. They are a great couple in our church, and they have a very specific foster-care ministry. They foster infants who are given up for adoption by their birthmothers while they are awaiting adoption. Often that means that Tim and Andra are the ones that bring these children home from the hospital and love and care for them over their first days and weeks while the process to move them on to their forever family is finalized. What they do amazes me. They don't change clothes in telephone booths or leap tall buildings in a single bound, but it takes a calling from God to have the strength to be willing to take on 2:00 A.M. feedings, changing diapers, mountains of laundry, and falling in love with a child that you know you will be passing along to a forever family, yet they do it with joy time and time again. I hope you enjoy hearing a little bit of their story and God's work in their lives. And, I hope you see that God and work in your life this way too. Tim and Andra aren't exceptional. They are just called and obedient, and we are thankful for their friendship and their example.

These ideas really only scratch the surface of how the church can respond to the foster care crisis we face today in America. No doubt, we have discovered and will discover endless ways to respond to the fatherless in our communities. Let us establish a goal. Let us work toward the goal that every child in our communities finds a place of love and safety to grow up. Let us dedicate ourselves to the goal that every child in our community has the opportunity to know Jesus and to feel His love through the actions of His church.

— RM

WHO ARE WE,
THAT YOU WOULD BE MINDFUL OF US?

A FOSTERING STORY—TIM AND ANDRA NETTLETON

*A*s I began to ponder this, that the Lord of all creation would be mindful of me, my heart began to ask, what can I do in a tangible way to serve Him? Just as the body is dead without breath, so also faith is dead without good works (James 2:26).

We have all been given different talents and abilities to serve Him. Mine happens to be caring for infants. No, I am not an RN or a pediatric nurse and have no special training other than what the Lord has put in me! For so long my heart asked, *But, Lord, why can't I sing; but, Lord, why can't I teach?* If only I knew the incredible blessings He had in store for me as I began to care for orphans. Pure and genuine religion in the sight of God the Father means caring for orphans and widows in their distress and refusing to let the world corrupt you (James 1:27).

Almost six years ago, my husband and I began the process of becoming an interim-care family with Bethany Christian Services in Hattiesburg, Mississippi. We quickly realized that our children were too young for us to care for them as we wanted and also foster infants. Our hearts were confident that waiting was the right thing to do. Fast-forward six years and we cannot begin to tell of the joys that the Lord has allowed us to have.

Knowing You Jesus, knowing You, there is no greater thing. You're my all. You're the best. You're my joy, my righteousness, and I love You, Lord!

We have had the honor and joy of caring for five infants in the past year. Some we have had for six weeks, others as little as two weeks. The first question we always get is, Is it hard to let them go? My answer is a resounding yes. Knowing we are loving these precious babies with the love of the Lord makes it all possible. Knowing we are attending angels unaware fills our home and hearts with a love made possible only by Him.

— TNA

It is a completely foreign thought to me to be 16 years old and on my own without support.

8

HOW DO YOU PROVIDE
TRANSITIONAL ASSISTANCE?

J have had a fascination with NASA and the space program for as long as I can remember. One of my favorite stories about the space program is the one retold in the 1995 movie *Apollo 13*. You remember the story—three American astronauts are put at risk after an accidental explosion aboard their spacecraft. The tireless effort and ingenuity of the NASA team creates a plan to bring the astronauts home safely. Against all odds, the plan works and the three men arrive home safely. It's a great movie, but it's an even greater story! Of all the amazing scenes in the movie, one stands out to me in particular. It's the scene when the engineers in Mission Control determine that the "scrubber" that cleans carbon dioxide out of the spacecraft's atmosphere has failed. They have to find a solution or the astronauts will die. What comes next is so cool! A group of engineers is assembled to take on this enormous task. Their leader dumps a box of expendable parts (OK, let's call it what it is . . . a box of junk) in front of them and tells them that they must use this junk to figure out a way to make a round filter fit a square hole, and failure is not an option.

Wow! What a story. What's even crazier is this really happened, and they actually solved the problem! As we approach the problem of orphans who must transition away from institutions into independent life as adults, I think we might feel a little like those NASA engineers. The problem seems insurmountable.

We look at the resources available to us compared to the scope of the problem and feel helpless. How can we make a difference in such a huge, complex situation with the little bit of money and time we have?

I also am drawn to think of a meeting that happened much closer to home. It happened only recently with Tasha, the director of recruiting and training for our local branch of Children's and Family Services. We were discussing how our church could be more meaningfully involved in the lives of fatherless children in our own community. We were talking about the difficulty that children face when they transition out of foster care into independence. In the middle of the discussion, Tasha uttered a sobering thought and her words cut like a knife. "If we fell on our faces, we had a place to go back to. These kids have no safety net. It might be when they are 15 or 16 in a foreign country or 18 or 21 here, but there comes a time when they are on their own with no margin for error and that's really very hard."

I must admit that it is a completely foreign thought to me to be 16 years old and on my own without support. No one to count on to love or help me.

My wife and I are in the process of adopting two more children, two teenage girls who will face life outside the orphanage if God doesn't grant us the grace to accomplish our mission. My heart hurts when I think about the thousands who don't have a mama and a papa who are coming to rescue them. Sadly, thousands of orphaned children face that reality every day. They are cast out of the only home they have ever known with no alternate plan. They are among the most vulnerable people walking the face of the earth. They have little option to provide for themselves, and the forces of darkness that would prey on their plight for selfish gain are around every turn.

God has called us to be a defender of the defenseless because that is who He is. We are returning worship to God when we show His character to the world by championing the cause of the least of these.

TRANSITIONS, SEXUAL SLAVERY, AND TRAFFICKING

*I*n 2010, the connection between human trafficking, sex slavery, and orphan transitions came to the forefront of the world's stage as the World Cup was held in South Africa. As the world descended on South Africa to compete together in an international sporting event, predators also descended bringing scores of young women to work in the brothels of South Africa during the event.

Literally thousands of young women were enslaved and smuggled against their will into South Africa to serve as prostitutes in the "entertainment" industry that supported the games. Many of these enslaved women were girls of no more than 12 or 13 years old. Impoverished families sold some into slavery while others were orphans who were abducted from orphanages or from the streets. Sadly, this type of orphan victimization is not just a result of occasional sporting events. Brothels, sweatshops, organized crime, and other illegal enterprises prey on orphaned children's need to survive and lack of voice as a source of forced labor.

They have no standing. They have no voice. They have no rights, and no one is coming to their rescue. James 1:27 demands that we must! At least part of the solution to their rescue is to prevent their victimization by helping them move from childhood to adulthood without being cast aside or slipping through the cracks.

Like the engineers who worked on *Apollo 13*, we have no blueprint from which to build a solution to this problem, but we have to remember, we have something better. We have a guide for our action that is much greater than mere expertise or experience, the Holy Spirit. We have a mission that is defined by God Himself. We are to care for orphans in their affliction, and a great affliction that many of the world's orphans face is abandonment as they become adults. We must trust that the Spirit of God will lead us toward solutions.

> We have something better. We have a guide for our action that is much greater than mere expertise or experience, the Holy Spirit.

At this point, I would love to give you a four-point plan for how you and your church can help to successfully transition orphans from the orphanage into adulthood. The truth is that we ourselves are in the infancy of dealing with this question. What I do believe I can offer you are some insights we have discovered along the way as well as an offer to join us in tackling this difficult question. What I believe we can't do is be paralyzed by the difficulty or the enormity of the question.

So, where are we to begin? I will take my cue from another favorite experience with the "happiest place on earth." Several years ago, I had the privilege of doing some consulting with a church near Orlando, Florida. One of the people that I met during that project was a Disney "imagineer." What, you might ask, is an imagineer? So far as I can tell, being an imagineer is something unique to Disney. It's a great job, but it's a job that many people would shy away from because lots of people would tend to think it couldn't be done. Imagineering is a job title that comes from Walt Disney's blending of the words *imagination* and *engineering* because those are the two essential skills that are necessary for those men and women entrusted with building the Disney theme parks. You see, Disney isn't satisfied with repeating an experience that has already been created. They put a premium on imagining something that has never been done before and then finding a way to do it. Disney wants you to experience things in their theme parks that are unique and set their parks apart from any other place in the world. Their goal is to be distinctively creative so that we will want to come back and vacation with them time and time again.

Their goal may be good, but it isn't of eternal value. How much more should that kind of creativity and confidence that is true of Disney be true of the church since we have been given all that we need for the work of God's kingdom? I would challenge you to take the following observations, pray, dream, and work toward creating solutions that do not yet exist for the good of orphans and the glory of God!

While there isn't a kit that you or your church can purchase that can give you a set of steps to undertake to solve the orphan transition problem, here are a few operating values/directions that you can instill in your ministry to begin to address the plight of older orphans who are transitioning out of their institutions.

FIRST, WE HAVE TO WORK TO STRENGTHEN THE TIE BETWEEN LOCAL CHURCHES AND ORPHANAGES.

Short of adoption, it is a must to have Christians investing regularly in the lives of orphans as mentors and life coaches. These kids need people who will build relationships with them and journey with them through life. Sadly, we have experienced a huge disconnect between the local church and the orphan in other places in the world just as has occurred here at home. Not long ago, I sat with an influential Ukrainian pastor brother who wept as he told me of the disinterest in the orphans and the street children of their country among his fellow pastors and their churches. It's not that I am pointing fingers at Ukrainian pastors or their churches. In many established US churches, we are struggling with the same inattentive spirit. One answer may lie in the church-planting movement that continues to sweep the globe.

Earlier in the book, we observed a connection across the world between church planting and orphan ministry. Some of the most exciting ministries springing up within nations to minister to institutionalized children and street children are from church plants. Tony and I have had the privilege over the last several years to serve as visiting professors in the church-planting program at the Kyiv Theological Seminary (KTS) in Ukraine. The young men whom we have taught as part of that program are required to plant a church before they can graduate from the seminary (how's that for a final exam?!). One of the interesting things that we have observed is the number of them that have acute awareness for the poor, the widow, and the orphan. They are planting churches who seek to live out James 1:27 from their very DNA. I would call on you and your church to support the training of church planters who carry the gospel to the unreached peoples of the world with the care and compassion of Christ and to provide for church-planting efforts among the nations that have orphan care as a component of their strategy.

> They are planting churches who seek to live out James 1:27 from their very DNA.

New churches hold great promise to assimilate orphans into their midst as part of their strategy because this is not a change in ministry philosophy, but that is not to say that we cannot foster that tie with orphans and existing churches as well. Tony did a great job of dealing with how we can lead churches to minister to orphans in chapter four, but we must also emphasize orphan ministry among the churches to whom we minister in our missional partnerships globally. Remember the Ukrainian pastor that I mentioned earlier. During one of our visits, we put it together that his wife had led a group of ladies who had visited my son in his orphanage. As the pastor of a long existing congregation, he was committed to changing the culture of the church. As I have discovered through our relationship, he is also a pastor who is dedicated to helping his church develop a heart for the nations. Not surprisingly, those two passions tend to run together. Being involved in supporting missions among the nations means exporting a missional zeal to our brothers and sisters around the globe that encourages them to see their world (both near and far) in terms of the pure and undefiled faith that is expressed by James in his letter to the church.

At this writing, I will soon leave with a team to head for Ukraine to work alongside one of the KTS church planters, Sergey, who is working toward a church plant. Sergey has a great strategic plan in place. He is reaching the families of his village at least in part through their children. His church is young. They just baptized their first two converts. Our role as a team, to support this fledgling church, is to raise awareness for their ministry by teaching English as a foreign language, and to assist their church-planting team in the work they have begun in a local orphanage and in food distribution to local widows. Why? Sergey is teaching his church to live missionally in their own community, and they are responding to James 1:27 in very practical ways from their founding as a church. The plan is simple. People want their children to learn English so that they can have an opportunity for a better life. English is a ticket to a better life. This part of the country does not often see many Americans.

Our other significant assignment is to spend every afternoon in the local orphanage. Sergey wants us to work with the orphans because that is his passion too. We really clicked when I taught his evangelism class recently. He wants to make a statement to his church and the community from the very beginning. Bringing a team from the US is a significant resource to him, and he wants to invest it into the fatherless and the oppressed! He takes James 1:27 that seriously. He wants caring for the hurting to never be separated from telling the Good News that Jesus came to set us free. That is church planting I can embrace!

Another possible gift that the US church could send to the nations is missionary social workers to work among the poor and the oppressed to spread the gospel and to care for them in their misery. Sadly, it seems that US churches and denominations have become increasingly disconnected from the practice of social work. While the practice of social work, like any social-science discipline, has the potential to fall prey to theological liberalism and to corrupt the gospel, there is no shame in meeting the needs of people in the name of Jesus (Matthew 25:31–40). Let me be clear. We need Christian social workers! We need Christians who are trained to mobilize us as to how to use our resources to ease the suffering of the masses of orphans, widows, and homeless people who are all around us. We need Christian social workers that can oversee cases and do home studies to facilitate adoptions here in the US. We need Christian social workers that can supervise and train foster families and can work with families of origin to help in healing them. And, we don't just need these social workers here. They are badly needed in places around the globe where they are less likely to be able to be afforded than in the US.

The dream is huge. To see it happen, we will need young people to answer the call to care for the poor. We will need colleges and seminaries to train workers. We will need people of means to fund these college and seminary programs (right now, New Orleans Baptist Theological Seminary has such a program ready to launch but the funds to launch it are lacking). And, we will need mission-sending agencies that will send these workers out and support them in their work. This is a huge goal, but there is a huge opportunity. Most of the developing world is underserved socially and Christian social workers sent by nongovernmental relief organizations have the potential to take the gospel to the nations by providing much needed and much asked for help.

ESTABLISHING A CONNECTION BETWEEN ORPHAN MINISTRY AND MISSIONAL ENTREPRENEURIALISM

The concept of business as mission is as old as the Bible itself. Missional entrepreneurialism involves Christians going to the nations to plant their lives among the peoples of the nations, creating for-profit businesses while also generating opportunities to live and share the gospel from within the culture. Recently, a movement has begun to gain momentum in the evangelical church called business as mission (BAM). These BAM entities could be founded with the intention of hiring orphan graduates, to give them a place to apprentice at a living wage while being protected from the predators who seek to pray on their vulnerable life state.

Most of my direct experience with orphaned kids has been in Ukraine, and most of the orphan care that we have witnessed there is in large, government-run institutional care. One large downside to the institutional model of orphan care is that the children are often not progressively equipped for life beyond the institution, as a child would be if she were raised in a typical family. Until the day she is put out onto the street, most of an orphan girl's schedule is not for her to decide. Someone else decides when she will get up, what she will eat, what she will do, and where she will go. She is given little opportunity to develop skills of independent thought. Her basic needs are met. She has food, clothing, and shelter, but she is not really being prepared for the day that will come when someone will tell her that it is time for her to leave. For the girls that are fortunate enough to have completed their secondary education while in the orphanage, the government will give them a place to live and a modest pension while they attend a trade school at the government's expense. That sounds great, right? However, that teenage girl—who has never had to wake herself up, take care of her own schedule, cook for herself, shop for herself, manage money for herself, or had a parent to show her how to do so—is now responsible for all that and no one is there to help.

Most don't figure it out and fall through the cracks where the pimps and the dealers are all too ready to pick them up and take them. What if the church sent short-term missionaries to orphanages that house older children, to teach these specific skills? We could establish partnerships to teach these kids about how to do basic living skills like cooking, cleaning, basic repair and maintenance, basic finance. We could take trips to ride public transportation and go on outings to help them learn the skills of polite conversation and proper etiquette. We could teach basic health and hygiene and planning for the future. There are ministries who are making strides in this area. In chapter 5, I introduced a ministry called Lifesong for Orphans. In addition to their great work in their Constant Christian Presence (CCP) initiative in a number of Ukrainian orphanages, they have begun programs to provide a home for children who "age-out" of the government-run orphanage system.

Their plan involves local churches providing support and accountability for these orphan graduates. Lifesong provides a stable home and lasting relationships through regular Bible study, counseling, and transportation to church activities by the Lifesong CCP staff. If you are interested in learning more about Lifesong for Orphans and their ministry, check out its Web site at www.lifesongfororphans.org.

The final idea for transitional assistance is perhaps the most simple of all (and it is the least original). We live in a technologically advanced age. Just this morning, I had the opportunity to talk to a missionary friend who is literally halfway around the world. Just a few years ago that conversation would have been impossible, and today it is routine. I got this idea from my friend Valerie Hall. They have purchased prepaid cell phones for the orphan graduates who have visited their home and from time to time they are able to provide time to these young people's phones. It is a lifeline. It is a message. It says someone cares. Someone is here. Someone is listening. Will you listen?

The truth is, we are groping for answers as to how to help institutionalized children transition well into adulthood. As a guy who has spent the better part of the last 20 years ministering to young people in the US, I realize that launching young people into the independence of adulthood is difficult even when the conditions are great. For institutionalized children, the conditions are poor and the stakes are high, but we must not fail. God's love for them compels us. He loves them and Jesus is worthy of their worship! I am looking forward to the creative discussions that will ensue. Let the prayer and the work begin. May God grant us the grace to see His kingdom's work accomplished! May the orphan be cared for and may the Father of all the fatherless be praised forever and ever! Amen!

— RM

A Personal and Transitional Ministry Testimony: The Homes of Hope for Children Story—Michael Garrett

*I*n many ways, it seems strange to be writing the story of Homes of Hope for Children since we just began serving children on July 12, 2010. However, as I thought about the many challenges of building our ministry during the past four years, it occurred to me that our experiences could serve as a source of encouragement for those who are called to begin a ministry. Instead of sharing a story with the proverbial happy ending, our story ends with a happy beginning. I believe that God's people need to be encouraged because He is calling all of us to accomplish great things for Him. The challenge we encounter is that Satan works hard to derail the plans that God has for us. However, sometimes it is in Satan's act of sabotage that God's Will is ultimately discovered. That is exactly how the vision for Homes of Hope for Children came about.

The Homes of Hope for Children vision has been a journey that began in 1987 when my sisters and I came to live at the Louisiana Baptist Children's Home. My first day on campus was a struggle as I tried to find the courage not to break down in tears. At that time, I did not know what a wonderful opportunity the Louisiana Baptist Children's Home would be for me and that God would one day use me to lead an effort to start a similar ministry for children in south Mississippi. However, God *did* know, and as it often happens, He uses the very things that were meant to destroy us to do His will and to help others. As I grew up at the Baptist Children's Home, unbeknownst to me God was teaching me important aspects of the ministry. He was helping me to develop the Homes of Hope for Children vision even as the Baptist Children's Home was meeting my needs. Shortly after graduating from high school, God called me to serve in children's home ministry. I felt God was calling me to spend the rest of my life making sure that other children received the same opportunity that I was given. I had no idea that the calling placed upon my heart would eventually lead me to south Mississippi to build Homes of Hope for Children. However, that was God's plan for my life, and I am thankful that He revealed His plan to me one small step at a time.

In June of 2006, I moved to south Mississippi with my wife, Julie, and my one-year-old son, Caleb, to build a children's home for boys and girls who were in need of a place to call "home." It was almost four years later that we welcomed the first children to our ministry. During that time, we faced many tough decisions and challenges. At times, it seemed that the only way for us to move forward was to simply fall forward. It is amazing to see how close we came to failing, but God's grace pulled us back from the brink every time. Being new to the area and having no contacts to begin sharing my vision, I turned to the Yellow Pages in our local phone book. I called local business owners who featured Christian fish symbols and Scripture verses in their ads. This led to many opportunities to share the Homes of Hope for Children vision with business leaders in our community. God blessed each meeting, and more and more speaking opportunities presented themselves. I began speaking to business groups and civic organizations, which led to speaking engagements in Sunday School classes. These opportunities eventually led to invitations to preach in our local churches, and it seemed that we were making new friends and supporters everywhere we went.

In February 2007, we found 42 acres in Purvis, Mississippi, that we felt would be the perfect location for our children's home. Taking a step of faith, we signed a contract in April that would allow us four months to raise $230,000. This challenge seemed nearly impossible since we had only raised a total of $110,000 for the entire year of 2006. During the next four months, God grew our faith and blessed our ministry. In August, with one final gift from the Lowrey family, Homes of Hope for Children was able to purchase the land. Over the next 18 months, we spoke to anyone who would listen to the Homes of Hope for Children vision and raised enough funds to complete the land development, roads, and infrastructure, and to build our first building.

On March 10, 2009, Homes of Hope for Children broke ground on our first building. Before the construction began, a local business owner, David Dearman approached me about utilizing volunteers to save money. I was concerned about finding volunteers that held the specific construction skills that we needed. However, God brought us a group of volunteers that possessed the exact skills that were needed to build our campus. It began with Jeremy Williamson, owner of Solid Rock Construction, who donated the forming and framing of our first building. Jeremy led us to many other contacts in the construction field that were able to either donate their services or give us a deep discount. Our local building supply companies ensured that we received the materials that we needed at a great price. We were blessed to have individuals like Mike Robinson with Probuild and Lance Myrick with Economy Supply who made sure that we had the materials we needed to keep the construction moving forward.

Even with this support, Homes of Hope for Children found itself about $250,000 short from being able to complete our first cottage and commissary, which needed to be finished before we could begin serving children. It was at this time that I learned about the Pepsi Refresh Project, a national contest in which voters decided which organizations would win a grant from Pepsi. We applied for a $250,000 grant and began competing on March 1. We needed to finish the month in the top two positions out of 288 competing organizations. Our community came together to help our little children's home ministry in Purvis, Mississippi, win a national competition for $250,000. With the grant, we were able to complete construction on our first cottage and commissary and begin serving children on July 12, 2010.

Since we began serving children, we have had many visitors on campus who are amazed at what has been accomplished in such a short time. The first question is usually, How did you do it? The answer to that question is easy for me: I didn't do it. God did it, and He used His people to make it happen. He did it with several thousand volunteer hours, many professional and nonprofessional volunteers, donated materials, donated food to feed the volunteers, church groups, civic organizations, college groups, youth groups, children's ministries, missions teams, and, most importantly, the prayers of His people crying out for a ministry to help hurting children who simply need a place to call home. Praise God! He has answered our prayers and the prayers of the children who are now living on our campus. To the readers of this book who have been a part of making Homes of Hope for Children a reality, I want you to know how much we appreciate your prayers and support. God has used you to accomplish something great. He has used you to not only make a generational impact but an eternal impact.

My prayer is that the Homes of Hope for Children story serves as a source of encouragement for those who are struggling to accomplish something great that God has placed upon their hearts. I was told along the way that the vision was unrealistic, and it often seemed the biggest challenge was just keeping the vision intact. As tough times hit and the mountain seems too steep, the temptation is to decrease expectations and standards. I encourage you to adhere to what the Lord has called you to do. There are those in need that are counting on you, and God has called you to meet their needs. Current events, a bad economy, or any other obstacle that is placed in front of you does not surprise him. Keep moving forward, even if it requires at times to simply fall forward.

— HHF

He felt the kind of love
that can only come from God
through His people.

9

HOW DO YOU DO ORPHAN-HOSTING MINISTRY?

In the preceding chapters, we have discussed the enormity of the world's orphan problem. You can see that no one approach is sufficient in our quest to live out James 1:27. The longer we pondered the problem, we became convinced that living out James 1:27 in today's world was going to call for innovation and an entrepreneurial spirit. The church has to be open to possibilities and strategies that are far beyond the norm if we are to make an impact.

As we searched for out-of-the-box ways of caring for orphans, I was drawn to an idea that was being carried out by some good friends in Birmingham, Alabama. Valerie and Randy Hall have been friends of the Morton family for a long time. God drew us together in multiple ways over the years while we have been friends. While I was in college, I became acquainted with Randy, who was the minister of youth at a large church in suburban Fort Worth, Texas. What began as a casual relationship with me serving as a retreat leader in Randy's ministry progressed into an internship within his ministry and many years later a collaboration in a Christian publishing company. We have had quite a ride with the Halls.

In addition to the ministry connection, Valerie and Randy have also served as a sort of "life guides" for Denise and me. You see, just about the time that we were being drawn to the decision couple of years before. Val and Randy were at that time adoptive parents of two precious girls. Their daughters were four and eight years old when they were adopted from Ukraine. Through the course of our first adoption, the Halls were a source of information and inspiration. Unbeknownst to them, God was using them in an even bigger way to shape our thinking about what could be done by a church to respond to James 1:27.

The Halls, like so many other adoptive parents, were profoundly shaped by their adoption experience, and you can find more of their story (including

the adoption of five more kids . . . *at once* . . . later in this chapter). While they were grateful for the girls God had brought into their family, the thousands who would not find a home burdened them. Who would give them hope? In 2004, the Halls and several other adoptive families in the Birmingham, Alabama, area formed an organization that would come to be known as Reach Orphans with Hope. The goal for Reach Orphans with Hope is found on their Web site (www.reachorphanswithhope.org):

"There are hundreds of thousands of 'human beings' . . . 'real people' who live out their childhood years with no mom and dad. Not having a mom and dad is just a small part of being an 'orphan.' The real pain of being an orphan comes from living your life under a banner of being REJECTED, UNWANTED, and OPTIONAL. These scars are worn deep within every orphan child, and the hurt does not go away when they turn 18. The value and self-worth issues continue . . . for life. Our most effective response is to LOVE THEM.

Christ was clear. He mentioned orphans specifically as a way to practice pure ministry. Those of us who serve through Reach Orphans with Hope are responding to this challenge with love, by inviting orphan children to visit us, by teaching and training them in preparation for life, and by traveling to their home in the orphanage to spend time with them in their world."

To achieve their goal, Reach Orphans with Hope began to capitalize on the common practice in Eastern European orphanages of sending children away to camps for the summer. Instead of letting some of these kids be sent to in-country camps, Reach Orphans with Hope invited them to come to Birmingham for a multiple-week camp experience.

During these camps, older orphan children are given an opportunity to experience things like fishing, swimming, riding bicycles, visiting museums, and many other activities that were likely beyond the scope of their lives in the institution. The most important thing they receive is unconditional love and hope. This hope is one that can only come from knowing that they are loved and valued by God, and it is delivered through people who are His.

In the summer of 2008, I led a small team from our church to Birmingham to spend a couple of days helping the Reach Orphans with Hope team in their hosting program. What we experienced changed our lives. We saw dozens of volunteers from churches throughout the Birmingham area loving and serving these orphan guests. We saw children who had arrived days earlier as timid strangers becoming part of a larger community of love. We saw orphanage workers, who were being ministered to by the love and care of Christian men and women, begin to see themselves and their vocations differently. And, we saw another avenue that God could use in our church to care for orphans.

On the van ride home, our team talked about what we experienced. The sentiment was unanimous, "With God's help, we can do this. We must do this!" God had to lead us to one of those Numbers 13 kinds of moments. We were either going to be the spies that saw the promised land with all of its challenges and still trusted God to lead us forward, or we were going to be the spies who saw orphan hosting as a good thing that was just too difficult for us. The challenge that lay before us was immense. How could we possibly muster up the people, money, and resources necessary to bring a group of kids halfway around the world? How could we negotiate the red tape of two governments to be allowed to bring kids to such a camp? Frankly, we didn't have answers to any of those questions. What we had was the example of others that it was possible and the confidence that God was leading us to pursue orphan hosting. After all, with Him all things are possible.

Promise 139

*O*ur original little "group of spies" began meeting to pray and talk in August of 2008. By late fall, we had a plan. We would begin to promote the idea of an orphan-hosting program in our church and community, and we would plan to host our first group of kids from Ukraine in the summer of 2010. By October, we had a pathway. Through an exciting connection between our church and an organization that provides a biblically based values curriculum to the public schools in Russia and Ukraine, we were able to have the promise of children to attend our orphan hosting camp in the summer of 2009!

By Christmas, we had a name, Promise 139. Our objective was simple. We wanted to use hosting orphans from around the world as a means for sharing hope with them from the seven promises found in Psalm 139:

1. God knows me. (v. 1)
2. God knows where I go. (vv. 2 and 3)
3. God knows my thoughts. (v. 4)
4. God has put His hand on me. (v. 5)
5. God is always with me. (vv. 7–12)
6. God has made me. (vv. 13 and 14)
7. God has made me unique. (v. 15)

As the spring of 2009 unfolded, we were still lacking two important ingredients: volunteers and money. What we found over the next three months is something we already knew—God provides the resources for His work in abundance. By the time our first camp rolled around, we had been able to raise well more than the $25,000 necessary to host our first group of orphan guests. We also saw more than 200 people from both our church and community embrace the vision and volunteer to be part of Promise 139. God lavished on us His plan in abundance.

Even with all of these victories, the road was not easy. Getting two national governments to play well together was a challenge. Getting visas processed and issued was challenging. With a great deal of prayer and too many international phone calls and emails to count, we finally secured the permission of both governments, and our orphan guests made their way through four flights, seven time zones, and across a cultural divide that is unimaginable.

When they arrived, we found six tired, timid children between the ages of 8 and 18. They and their stories were incredibly varied. There was a brother and sister who were abandoned to the orphanage when their mother died. One boy, 15 years old, was removed from his mother's care after years of horrible neglect. This kind and polite young man had been robbed of even the chance to attend school until he was placed in the orphanage as a teenager. There was the teen girl who stood off—shy but curious. She bore the wounds of severe disappointment. There was the little jokester whose 11-year-old body barely seemed big enough for his smile. And then there was the baby, a reserved little 8-year-old boy whose smile we would find out in the days to come had never even been seen by his orphanage director. They were here, and for two weeks, they were ours to love and to be shown the Savior.

> What I liked the most were the people I met here and how they work together and love each other. I'm not used to seeing that.

What an amazing two weeks it was. God granted favor, and the kids came out of their shells. Through it all, they learned about God and His love and care for them through the lives of ordinary people who love Jesus. We had two crazy weeks full of lots of joy. We swam, rode horses, played games, ate meals, and did many things together. Near the end of the two weeks of camp, someone asked one of the older kids what his greatest memory was, and you might be surprised at his answer.

He did not say the trip to a professional baseball game or the birthday party that our volunteers threw them. He did not say the house they lived in or any of the restaurants where they ate. He said, "What I liked the most were the people I met here and how they work together and love each other. I'm not used to seeing that." He went on to say, "I haven't really ever thought much about the future before now, but now I am. I want to make plans for my life."

That's how *hope* sounds. He experienced unconditional love. He felt the kind of love that can only come from God through His people. God was wrapping His arms around this young man through the obedience of His church, and this hurting child was responding. For the first time in his life, he believed he had a future and a loving Father he could trust for that future.

Orphan Hosting 101

*F*rom time to time, we have had people ask why we would go to such a great extent to bring these kids to our country or why we don't just focus on the needs in our own community. First, I would say that we do focus on the needs in our own community. This book details the importance of local ministries. Not to be locally involved in orphan care would be disobedient to Jesus and His command to be His representatives in Jerusalem (home), Judea and Samaria (our country), and to the ends of the earth (the nations). But, to focus only on our local areas and disregard the needs of the nations would be equally disobedient. We must do both.

Second, taking kids out of the familiar context of their orphanages and giving them an experience like international travel can be an element of fostering hope. Helping them to see the world as bigger and more hospitable than the world of their experience can be a great source of encouragement. Dangling the promise of hope before a child who has none can also be a crushing blow. Orphan hosting is about living the gospel and showing hope to these children in the long run. Once we meet these children through hosting, they become our responsibility. If we do not intend to stay connected to the kids we host, then we should not host at all. To be given a taste of a future but not be encouraged and supported as you try to move toward it is perhaps worse than never being given a taste at all. We do not want to embitter these children; we want to continue to love them and remind them that they are not alone because they have us, and more importantly, they have Jesus.

A bonus benefit of orphan hosting is the increasing of adoption awareness and in it—motivating adoption. Although our focus in hosting children is not adoption, some of the children who visit may be pursued for adoption. As of the writing of this book, five of the first six children hosted by Promise 139 are being pursued for adoption. International adoption is an uncertain process. We do not know what the future will bring and whether these children will find families in our community. We are hopeful, and we pray for each of them to find a forever family.

Adoption awareness is also increased as people meet these children. Most of the volunteers with Promise 139 have never visited an orphanage and many have never even met an orphan. Repeatedly, I have had people express the same startling sentiment to me about the orphans we host. They say things like,

"You know, they are just kids. Kids just like ours." Yes, they are, but meeting them takes the anonymity away and calms the fear that many have when they think about older orphans and their needs. Over and over, orphan-hosting groups have seen people who have not ever considered adoption begin to pray about God's desire for them to adopt as a result of meeting an orphan and building a relationship with him or her.

So, if you were to consider orphan hosting as a ministry, here are a few suggestions to consider.

CREATE AN ENTITY APART FROM YOUR CHURCH FOR ORPHAN HOSTING.

*O*rphan hosting is an opportunity to get the church involved in orphan ministry across local church and even denominational boundaries. We have seen Promise 139 grow a broad base of support throughout the churches of our community. Hosting is a big undertaking and so is cultivating awareness for ministry to the fatherless. The task is too large for only one church, and including lots of churches in orphan hosting is a great way to address both objectives. Another potential reason to constitute as an entity separate from the church is the reluctance of other national governments to release children into the care of churches. Many of the nations that allow children to travel outside their country for hosting opportunities have informal yet strong church-state ties. The goal of orphan hosting is not to make Baptists or Methodists of the children; it is to show them hope in Christ.

MAKE A PLAN FOR YOUR ORGANIZATION THAT IS BOTH STRATEGICALLY SOUND AND SPIRITUALLY CENTERED.

*F*rom the very beginning, you need to be planning for the future. There is an adage that goes something like this, "As the work begins, so it will go." When beginning an orphan-hosting program (or any parachurch ministry for that matter), paying attention to details and thinking into the future as you begin will save you much angst down the road. As you bring a group together to consider hosting, clarify your common mission, long-term vision, essential values, and so on. In establishing a ministry entity (most probably a nonprofit ministry corporation), don't just think about the strategic decisions either.

Satan is a deceiver and a divider. He does not want us to spread the gospel or to redeem the orphan. Over the two years we have been hosting orphans, we have seen spiritual warfare in a big way. Being transparent, much of that warfare has been in the relationships we enjoy between the people who are part of Promise 139, and it's not just us. As I have talked to others who host, they tell the same story. Satan seems to have a strategy, and he's a master at using it. How do we combat it? We pray, and we try to live in our working relationships according to how the Bible presents reconciliation and relationships within the body of Christ. From the Bible, God is honest with us. If we work together and live in close proximity as men and women who are struggling to grow to be like Jesus, we are going to offend each other, sin against each other, and have our tough times relationally. The emotional nature of orphan hosting seems to amplify some of these issues. Always remember, Satan is the enemy, never the others who love orphans but disagree with your approach to ministering to them. We must be committed to putting on the armor (Ephesians 6:10–19) God provides as work together to care for orphans.

SEEK PARTNERSHIPS WITH INTERNATIONAL ORPHAN MINISTRY ORGANIZATIONS.

*O*ur connection to begin our ministry in Ukraine came through another established ministry. We didn't have a presence in another country. We didn't know any orphanage directors or other people who could facilitate those relationships. By partnering with organizations that were already engaged in international orphan care, we were able to avoid what could have been a years-long process of meeting and gaining favor and trust with the officials who we would work with to host kids. These partner organization were able to "pass the blessing" of trust and credibility to us and, in return, our work and integrity brought greater credibility to them in the eyes of their international constituents.

IF POSSIBLE, CONSIDER HOSTING ORPHAN GROUPS TOGETHER IN ONE HOME.

I have often tried to put myself in the place of a child who has just traveled halfway around the world to come be part of our orphan-hosting program. Any way you stack it, it has to be scary. I have also tried to put myself in the shoes of the orphanage director who is sending the children into the care of people that he or she barely knows. The director has a lot at risk. He is legally responsible for the children, and it takes a certain amount of faith to trust them into the care of strangers. Sure, we provide all kinds of insurance and other documentation to convince the director and his supervisors in government that we are responsible and trustworthy, but our assurances can only go so far. That is a major reason that we have decided it is best to host the groups in one location. That way, the director or his representative, who is the on-site official ultimately responsible for the children, is present with all the children all the time. I know of other hosting groups that split children up among several homes, but for the security of the children and the peace of mind of the director, it seems better to us if you can keep the entire group together to do so. The language barrier is difficult enough for us to negotiate, and I can't imagine how we could manage the chaos or get to a level of trust with the kids or the director if we were spread out into multiple homes. Also, keeping the program confined to one location helps us to maintain a level of accountability with our volunteers (background checks, house rules, etc.) that allows us to operate the ministry above reproach.

ORIENT ALL VOLUNTEERS AND VISITORS TO THE UNIQUE OPPORTUNITIES AND CHALLENGES OF ORPHAN HOSTING AND SCREEN THEM TO PROTECT THE KIDS IN YOUR CARE.

We have found that having a mandatory orientation and training for all of the folks who will be interacting with the children is a must. During this orientation session, we explain the mission, purpose, and vision of Promise 139, including our position on adoption. In addition, volunteers are informed on issues such as house rules for the host home, ministry policies, daily schedules, and cultural nuances from the children's' country of origin that will be helpful in building relationships.

Several weeks before the hosting, we invite potential visitors and volunteers to a couple of orientation meetings to review these items and to prescreen these folks with the appropriate background-screening measures. These large group meetings help us to get the majority of our workers on the same page well in advance of the kids' coming so that we are able to hit the ground running when they arrive. For those who do not attend an advance orientation and training session, we have a quick, simple process to prepare them as well.

The host home property is set up so that volunteers and visitors must pass by a check-in station to sign in or out each time they arrive or depart. If a visitor comes for the first time, one of the Promise 139 board is assigned the responsibility to conduct an orientation session with them before they are allowed access to the camp. We also have the capability to run preliminary background screenings immediately from the host home. All of this may seem a bit strict, but these are similar procedures to those most churches have in place to protect children in their care, and we are convinced that this is an appropriate standard of care for orphan hosting as well. While we don't imagine predators hiding around every corner, we are aware that orphan visitors might seem to be an easy target for those who would seek to abuse children. These children have been hurt enough; therefore, we go to great lengths to protect them from being further victimized while they are in our care. Moreover, we have found that preparing volunteers and setting their expectations in advance really helps all of us live in the moment with the kids. We don't waste a great deal of time on getting everyone into the mechanics of the program and can focus more attention on loving the kids God has privileged us to host.

SOLICIT VOLUNTEERS WITH A WIDE RANGE OF ABILITIES AND EXPERIENCES.

The children that we host have a variety of interests and needs. The blessing of being part of the body of Christ is that God has given each of us different talents and abilities as gifts, and He has redeemed us so that we should use those gifts for His glory in the work of His kingdom. Orphan hosting gives an opportunity for many believers to use their gifts for totally selfless ends that give God much glory.

We have dentists and doctors who are followers of Jesus who donate their time and expertise to give care to kids who lack some of the basic care we take for granted. Along the way, we met a lady who can lead worship and knows Russian! What an incredible blessing that she was able to take those two seemingly unrelated gifts and put them together to lead orphaned children to praise Jesus. I remember watching as a group of ladies brought their hobby of scrapbooking and helped the children build memory books as a way of giving them a tangible gift of remembrance.

I think it is interesting that in Paul's first letter to the Corinthian church, his discussion of the body of Christ is sandwiched between his teaching on spiritual gifts and love. The context of his teaching gives us a great amount of insight into our mandate to act as Christians. In essence, what we see in 1 Corinthians 12 and 13 is like a spiritual algebra equation. We are to use the gifts that God has given us as part of the church to demonstrate to the world the love of God that was made evident in Jesus to the glory of God.

In the course of hosting orphans, we have seen this spiritual equation take root in the lives of over 200 believers. Many of them are not gifted to be teachers or leaders and have struggled to find a place to use their gifts in the church. So, we have seen a dual benefit. Love and the gospel shown through these folks enrich the lives of orphaned children, and many of these folks themselves are finding for the first time their role in service to God's kingdom!

PROMOTE ORPHAN HOSTING AS A GLOBAL MISSIONS OPPORTUNITY FOR ALL AGES.

One of the members of the Promise 139 board has said from the very beginning that a significant factor in her involvement in this ministry is the opportunity for her young children to be engaged in global missions. By far, this is not the most significant reason to host orphans and, like all missions opportunities, we don't need to do missions for how they will benefit us. Yet as we aid orphans in their distress, there is a corresponding benefit for people of all ages as they engage in the work of Christ. In a ministry like this, people of all ages are integral to showing and presenting the gospel to these kids.

> There is a corresponding benefit for people of all ages as they engage in the work of Christ.

The local children who are involved in our hosting program never cease to amaze me. While adults often become preoccupied with concerns like the language barrier, children simply play. To them, life is simple. Some of the greatest moments we have witnessed were born when our children "gave a cup of cold water in Jesus' name" to an orphan child in the form of unconditional love and acceptance. I am also grateful for the opportunity that orphan hosting has given to my then kindergarten- and first-grade-aged sons to live missionally and think globally at that stage of their lives instead of them having to wait until they were "old enough." I am so thankful that my boys have a picture of global missions that is not abstract or future-oriented. They are engaged in sharing Jesus with the nations, and I pray that the seeds that are planted in these early years will bear fruit in their commitment to Christ and to the nations for their entire lives.

FOCUS ON THE GOSPEL AS THE REASON FOR ORPHAN HOSTING.

*L*ike any other social ministry, orphan-hosting programs can easily become focused on good goals that are not the best goal. Continually, it must be reinforced to everyone that showing and sharing the good news of Jesus Christ and His love and His sacrifice for these children is our ultimate goal. Along the way, we want these kids to have fun, to experience things that they otherwise wouldn't, and to learn about our culture. We also want to give people in our own community an up-close experience with orphans, and we want to stretch our thinking about missions to include that everyone from preschoolers to senior adults can live missionally. These are all really good goals, but if we reach all of them and fail to lead these children toward finding their ultimate hope in Jesus, we have failed.

> If we are going to commit to these children, it must be for the long haul.

ESTABLISH CONNECTIONS THAT WILL ALLOW FOLLOW-UP WITH ORPHAN VISITORS ONCE THEY LEAVE.

*A*gain, hosting by itself is not enough. In fact, to bring these kids halfway around the world to shower them with love and to show them the promise of a better life both tangibly and spiritually without ongoing follow-up is both shortsighted and cruel. If we are going to commit to these children, it must be for the long haul, and committing for the long haul is no easy task. There are several practical ways that hosting programs can maintain that tie.

First, you can begin a pen pal program. Your ministry can offer the service of translating and forwarding messages to the kids. In the electronic age, this is an easy thing to do. We have found that because of limited Internet access by the orphan children and the translation problems, it is a little difficult for us to rely on direct email and Facebook as a conduit for contact. Since we are dealing with minors, by managing a pen pal program, we can ensure that all the communication is appropriate.

A second idea is to take James 1:27 quite literally, and visit these children in their affliction. By leading regular missions trips to the orphanage where these children live, we can continue to love and care for them. These missions trips can accomplish many purposes, including providing humanitarian aid (food and clothing), construction projects (particularly repair of facilities that are in disrepair as a result of inadequate funding), and discipleship (programs like Vacation Bible School or Backyard Bible Clubs). By going to them, we give evidence to these children of our ongoing love and support.

Another avenue of follow-up is to become active in helping these children become ready for the transition to life beyond the institution. I must admit that this is the most difficult and least-answered problem of follow-up that we have encountered. I only mention transitioning here as a way of linking this problem to that of follow-up. In the previous chapter, we took up the discussion of transitional assistance and it's role in orphan care.

FINALLY, KEEP YOUR DISTANCE FROM ADOPTION MINISTRY.

*A*doption is a by-product of orphan hosting, but it is not the central focus. Adoption and adoption talk can take over a hosting project if allowed. Kids need to have the freedom to come and be loved without feeling like they are on display. We often say to each other that we can never let the culture of an orphan-hosting program become "like a middle school dance." You know, that awkward feeling that everyone is looking around trying to figure out who they will take a risk on and ask to dance. Orphaned children are not a commodity, and we don't need to try to show them off like they are.

We would love to see every orphan adopted and loved by a family. The feeling is especially strong with regard to children that we meet and love personally. The fact is that hosting a group of orphaned children is an emotionally charged enterprise. People are sometimes overwhelmed by their empathy for the kids, and we can even be drawn out emotionally by the stress and fatigue that comes with a two-week camp experience. From time to time, people who meet these children feel compelled to consider things like the adoption of a child as an emotional reaction rather than as a prayerful course of action.

There is no shame in being emotional over the plight of an orphan, and we want people to wrestle with God's will for their lives concerning adoption, but we need to guard the hearts of these children. They have been disappointed enough. To that end, we ask all volunteers and visitors to our camp not to talk about adoption while they are at the camp. We take this issue very seriously. In fact, adoption talk (or using the A-word as we like to say) is one of the few reasons that someone will be asked to leave the host home and invited not to return.

As a way to minister to families who are impacted by the camp and want to explore adoption, we schedule a couple of evening meetings at an off-site location to give them an opportunity to ask questions about adoption and the adoption process and to interact with adoptive families. These meetings are also a great time both to pray and to help these families know that we are committed to walking with them as they explore whether or not to adopt. Also, as part of the orientation process for visitors and volunteers, we explain the policy on adoption-talk and make sure they are aware of our adoption-interest meetings.

Promise 139 is a ministry that continues to develop. We are still learning. If you have interest in orphan hosting, we would be delighted to share our experiences and the lessons we continue to learn along the way. You can learn more about Promise 139 at our Web site, www.promise139.org. We would love to hear from you and become part of your journey in orphan ministry and orphan hosting. Our greatest desire is to see many orphan-hosting programs spring up all over to host children from around the world to the glory of God for the advance of the gospel.

— RM

A HOSTING AND ADOPTION STORY: RANDY AND VALERIE HALL

"For I know the plans I have for you," declares the Lord,
"plans to prosper you and not to harm you, plans to give you hope
and a future. Then you will call on me and come and pray to me,
and I will listen to you. You will seek me and find me when
you seek me with all your heart."

—Jeremiah 29:11–13

$\mathcal{D}$uring some challenging days in 1992, Valerie and I together claimed the truth and promises of this verse. At that time we had been married for eight years, we had served in ministry together in churches, and we had started our family. God blessed us first with an amazing daughter, followed by two wonderful sons. We had no idea what would be revealed next over the following years in the way of God's blessings again.

In 1993, Student Life was birthed in the basement of our home. In 1998, Student Life Missions started as a way to support youth camp ministry in Ukraine. In 2000, we agreed together to begin to grow our family through international adoption, and in 2001, we brought home Hallie and Kristina to join Madison, Gray, and Connor into a "blended family."

In 2003, we were given an opportunity to host a group of older orphans in our home in Birmingham with the help of friends, church, and community. Reach Orphans with Hope was formed as a way to minister to orphans. In that same year of 2003, Student Life Publishing was formed to make way for the introduction of Student Life Bible Study. That journey continued as we began our second adoption process. This has been yet another step in our faith journey that is really about what God can do. As uncomfortable and unlikely as we feel sometimes with the journey, we know that it is our great privilege to have a front row seat as we enjoy watching and serving alongside others who have joined us along the way to see these ministries develop and grow and make a difference in people's lives.

> In 1993, Student Life was birthed in the basement of our home. In 2003, Student Life Publishing was formed.

We eventually brought five more children into our world and ultimately into a loving relationship with Jesus Christ. There are hundreds of thousands of "human beings" . . . real people who live out their childhood years with no mom and dad. Not having a mom and dad is just a small part of being an "orphan." The real pain of being an orphan comes from living your life under a banner of being "rejected, unwanted, and optional." These scars are worn deep within every orphan child, and the hurt does not go away when they turn 18. The value and self-worth issues continue...for life. Our most effective response is to *love* them.

Christ was clear. He mentioned orphans specifically as a way to practice pure ministry. Those of us who serve through Reach orphans With Hope are responding to this challenge with love, by inviting orphan children to visit us, by teaching and training them in preparation for life, and by traveling to their home in the orphanage to spend time with them in their world. One of our primary outreach focus areas includes:

ORPHANS VISITING THE US

*O*rphan children from Ukraine come to enjoy an experience love, life, and hope. Hundreds of volunteers come together for a few special weeks in the summer to donate their time, energy, and love to these special children from Ukraine. Through our Summer Orphan Program, we are able to bring orphan children, an orphanage guardian, and a translator for a once-in-a-lifetime experience. Volunteers come to our home setting to help with the meals, transportation, group outings, and to establish and build relationships with the children. Activities, such as swimming, going to the movie theater, visiting the science center, a talent show, and dress-up days are just some of the highlights of the children's time with us. They also receive dental and medical attention, establish forever friendships, and experience an overflow of unconditional love. The Summer Orphan Program is a great way for families and individuals to experience missions up close and personal. This is a life-changing experience.

Since 2003, we have brought almost 100 orphan children to our home and almost 50 of those children, aged 6 to 16, have been adopted or are in the process to be adopted.

All of the funds needed to bring groups over and supply their needs are raised through donations and community support.

There are opportunities to stay in touch with the kids through our Pen Pal Club and Outreach Trips to Ukraine and visits to the orphanages and children. Individuals' involvement makes an impact. Whether its preparing meals, washing clothes, loving on children, or donating resources, there's a place for everyone!

OUR DREAMS

*W*e would love to assist with more in-country projects for orphan graduates. The statistics speak for themselves and the grim future the orphan graduates face. We would love to be part of an orphan graduate center for developing life and job skills, state-of-the-art technology training, building self esteem, Bible study, developing art and music programs and more. We would love to help more families be directly involved in orphan outreach…whether through sponsorship of an orphan in Ukraine, humanitarian improvement efforts in orphanages and foster homes throughout Ukraine, or through forever families.

— VHR

When people ask me, "How do you want to be introduced?" I usually propose they say, 'This is Tim Keller, minister of the Redeemer Presbyterian Church in New York City.' Of course, I am many other things, but that is the main thing I spend my time doing in public life. Realize, then, how significant it is that the Biblical writers introduce God as a 'father to the fatherless, a defender of widows' (Psalms 68:4–5). This is one of the main things he does in the world. He identifies with the powerless, he takes up their cause.

—Tim Keller, *Generous Justice*

CONCLUSION

TONY MERIDA

*W*heels up in two hours." As I write these final paragraphs, my wife and I are beginning our trip from New Orleans to Ethiopia via New York and Cairo. We are headed to a country with reportedly more than 5 million orphans. I'm trying to prepare myself for the gripping images of abandoned children, hungry children, lonely children, disfigured children, unwanted children. We're taking with us two duffel bags of shoes to give away at the orphanage, hoping to provide a little joy and comfort to some children's lives. But there's so much more to do. And my heart breaks for these kids.

Even after adopting four kids, I'm certainly not an old pro at this. And I'm trying to prepare myself to meet our new son, Eyasu (Joshua). I haven't slept all week. I haven't been able to get the thought of his little smile out of my mind, especially the picture of him holding up a dry-erase board with *Merida* written below his name. We're taking him some new gear, like flip-flops, new clothes, toothbrush, coloring books, and, of course, a baseball glove.

I'll never forget seeing his picture for the first time. We read how his parents died when he was one and that he had no siblings. His uncle put him in the orphanage. He was referred to as a sweet child who is a "little helper."

We've received a few little three-minute videos of him playing and talking. He cracked his front two teeth recently, which makes his smile doubly cute to me. We can't wait to give him a new family, with a mama and papa and brothers and sisters.

Needless to say I'm eager to meet him! I'm full of emotion right now. I long to put my arms around this little guy. I want to father him the way God has fathered me and rescued me in my spiritual affliction. When I was an orphan, a slave, broken, separated from the Father, and spiritually alone, God sent Jesus on a rescue mission to make me a son of God. I pray that Joshua would come to know this Savior at a young age and serve Him with all his heart.

We wrote this book because there are more than 140 million Joshua's in the world today. I know I'll see some of them in a few days. In fact, the hardest part about adopting for me isn't living in a different country, eating different food, spending a lot of money, or rearranging some things in my home and life to make room for another child. The most heart-wrenching aspect of adopting Joshua will be leaving behind other kids. I still remember the day we left for Ukraine, and the sight of other wonderful children watching us drive away. It was a sobering reminder that the world is not as it should be.

Because we live in a fallen world, where kids are orphaned and oppressed, God's people have a lot of mercy ministry to do. I don't know where you are as you read this book. Perhaps you could pray about adopting. Maybe you want to start a ministry in the local church—an adoption fund or an orphan-hosting ministry. Whether it's these ministries, foster care work, transitional assistance, building orphanages, underwriting orphanages, paying for someone's adoption—my prayer is that you would *do something*.

I hope this book has helped you by providing some biblical foundations and practical insights for gospel-centered adoption and orphan care. Much more could be said about "orphanology." Certainly, all of the subjects related to the study of orphans have not been considered. Leonardo da Vinci said, "Art is never finished, it's only abandoned." This book is not finished. There's much more to be written. And the work of orphan care definitely is not finished either. May God help you as you find a way to add a stroke of mercy to the unfinished work of caring for the fatherless.

— TM

RICK MORTON

*A*s I pen my part of this conclusion, it is a quiet Saturday in the Morton house, and that is rare. I'll take it when I can. Our story, like Tony and Kimberly's, continues to unfold. We are waiting on permission from our government to go back to Ukraine to invite two teenage girls to join our family. One we have met, and the other we haven't. They have no idea we are coming. Ultimately, we don't know what they will say, we are just confident that it is God's plan that we are supposed to go ask. He's worked out every detail so far. Every question answered and every penny accounted for in His timing. It gives us great confidence.

It's crazy if you don't know our Father. If you haven't been adopted through our Brother, it sounds like lunacy. Even if you have, it still may! Just pray for us and love us. All we know is we are confident in God more than ourselves, and we are going. For now, the book has to be completed, but life is not. I hope that there will be time for an epilogue to give you the rest of the story. If not, there will always be a blog. Or better yet, maybe we can grab a cup of coffee and talk about how God is using us to care for the fatherless to the praise of His glorious grace! I would love that.

— RM

APPENDIX 1

A WORD TO MOTHERS

ON WAITING — *Denise Morton*

*W*hen people want to talk to me about adopting, sometime in the conversation they usually ask, "How long did the process take?" For us, I can answer easily: the first one, from the beginning until we traveled, took ten months; it took two-and-a-half years for the second one. (I'm hoping the current one will only take seven months to complete.) The response I usually get is, "Wow!"

Looking back, Erick's (the first one) process was more like a whirlwind, although it didn't seem like it at the time. For his, we were somewhat naive. Early on, we circled a date on the calendar and said, "This is when we want to travel." Now, that was really arrogant on our part. But God is gracious and honored that for us, and we traveled on that date (with three days' notice). If Erick's process was a whirlwind, then Nicholas's was drudgery. It seemed most of the time that it would never happen, but we finally got the call for our appointment on Christmas Eve.

With both, waiting on the travel date was one of the hardest parts of the process. In talking with other adoptive parents, both domestic and international, that is a similar sentiment. Once all the paperwork is processed and you are either waiting on a birth mom match or a referral/appointment from a country, the waiting is miserable. It is then when your faith is essential, and you trust that God is sovereign and everything happens in His time.

After we were home with Erick for some time, I began to put together a timeline, beginning with the first mention of Ukraine until we traveled. I marvel at how God put people and things into motion before I was even aware or knew that there was a little boy who would need a family. When we did travel and get the referral for him, Erick had only been available for a couple of weeks. We didn't even have a picture of him before we traveled to the orphanage.

I don't know why we were delayed so long for Nicholas, and I doubt I'll ever know. He was in the orphanage for four years before we adopted him. He had gone through circumstances that raised his hopes and expectations, only to be hurt and discouraged. He needed time to heal and be ready to join his forever family. In many ways he didn't, and he is still adjusting from institutional life to family life. Again, this is when we trust in God's sovereignty and faithfulness to help us all.

Our current adoption is unlike the previous two. With the two others, we traveled not knowing how many, what age, or which gender. Ukraine doesn't give referrals until you are in the country. This time we met a shy, precious 13-year-old who came to the US as part of a Promise 139 camp. She stole my heart. Next to having to leave Erick in Ukraine for the 30-day appeal period (which has now been changed to 10 days), putting her on a plane to go back to her orphanage was the hardest thing I've had to do. Rick and I spent the next several months in prayer about adopting her and her 14-year-old sister. God kept drawing us to her over time. And now, we find ourselves in a familiar place—waiting.

If you are considering adoption or are in the adoption process, know that you are not alone. Others have gone through similar experiences; seek them out. They can be great sources of encouragement. Your social worker and/or adoption agency can also be encouragers. Most of all trust God and know that His timing is perfect.

—DM

MANAGING EXPECTATIONS — *Kimberly Merida*

> *Today is the day we have been waiting for since October 2007 when we first began our home study ... here we are approximately 18 months later. Lord, I confess my mind is racing with imaginations of what lies ahead. This is a little scary. Grant me grace and peace today I pray as we go forth. What an incredible privilege it is to walk in this journey of adoption parenting. Help me, Lord, today to focus, to be still, to hear Your voice. I know that You are ever-present ... You have prepared us for this day, this season. As I look to You in Your Word, show me Your glory ..."*

*I*t has been approximately 18 months since that momentous morning, the day the Lord revealed our children to us. I remember waking up the next morning with thoughts that shifted back and forth from funny to flat-out scary. What would our trip home look like? What would need to be done to our house to accommodate the children? How would I transition to cooking for six people instead of two? How much would our cost of living go up? Health insurance? Clothes? Would people think we were crazy? At that moment I knew that this adoption thing was so much bigger than me. I could not get Isaiah 55:8–9 out of my head, *"For my thoughts are not your thoughts, neither are your ways my ways, declares the LORD. For as the heavens are higher than the earth, so are my ways higher than your ways and my thoughts than your thoughts."* Your thoughts and expectations will no doubt run rampant. My advice to you is to confess them; write them down and then surrender them to the Lord who knows your needs and meets them according to His great mercy.

Sunday, 5/16/10

> *Today is our one-year anniversary of being home. I cried last night as I posted a blog with pictures from that day. Wow. God, You are so gracious to us! Today's Scripture reading is Proverbs 16. How fitting: "The plans of the heart belong to man, but the answer of the tongue is from the LORD. All the ways of man are pure in his own eyes, but the*

LORD weighs the spirit. Commit your work to the LORD and your plans will be established." Lord, I want to lay down all my plans before Your throne and commit them to You.

The first year home seems more of a blur than anything. It is amazing to reflect on where the Lord has brought our family in a relatively short amount of time. One thing is certain: God is faithful. I don't know exactly what I was expecting, but the grace of God carried us through. There were some glorious moments and some real painful moments. When you send your child up to their room, then go upstairs to join them in order to provide disciplined instruction on why their particular behavior was inappropriate only to find them crouched in the corner terrified that they will be beaten, it's almost more than the heart can bear. One thing is for sure I was not expecting to face symptoms of abuse and neglect, especially times four! Again, God has given us what we have needed each day. And each day, we have desperately depended on His sustaining grace to walk humbly as new parents.

Wednesday, 8/11/10

Today is the day we meet Eyasu. I confess my stomach is in knots, and I don't know if I'm ready for this. All I can do is ask, Lord, for Your ever-present help and wisdom and guidance as we prepare to meet. Reign over our time together. Be with our kids at home. Grant them peace. Speak peace to my stomach and my nerves. Thank you for the gift of motherhood. Help me love Eyasu and all our kids as You have loved me.

Going from zero to 5 children in 15 months is a challenge, which of course is the understatement of the year. I confess I was not one who grew up dreaming about being a mother. I just looked forward to being a wife and knew that God would grow a maternal desire in me when it was time. When we began the process, I was nervous about adopting two children under age five. I was secretly hoping we would start with one child like most families do. Now, I'm almost ashamed to admit that and can't imagine life being any different or more wonderful than it is now. What incredible joy it is to walk in what God has put before us, the honor of mothering five amazing children! It is hands down the hardest thing I've ever had to do in my life! It is also the greatest responsibility and weightiest honor I'll ever have.

One of the best pieces of advice I received was the warning not to expect your child or children to be grateful. It is in our nature to have this sort of savior complex where you want to say, "Can't you see we've *rescued* you from neglect, loneliness, and orphan status? Love me. Attach to me immediately. Appreciate me." When in reality, there is only one Rescuer, one Savior, and we want to do the same thing to Him—rebel. "*Rejoice in hope, be patient in tribulation, be constant in prayer*" (Romans 12:12).

Something that has been difficult is working to guard family time. Adopting older children means a lot of making up for lost time. Children have needs of their own. Everyone around you, family and friends, will want a part of you, as well as to offer their own parenting strategies. Set appropriate boundaries, and know your personal limits. Don't be afraid to tell others no. Don't feel the pressure to conform to what other adoptive families may be doing. You know your child's needs more than anyone. You also know your limits. In the end, here's the best advice I can offer, "*Trust in the LORD with all of your heart, and do not lean on your own understanding. In all your ways acknowledge him and he will make straight your paths*" (Proverbs 3:5–6).

—KM

APPENDIX 2

Resources

John Piper, "Adoption: The Heart of the Gospel" [sermon online]; available at www.desiringgod.org/ResourceLibrary/ConferenceMessages/ByDate/2007/1991_Adoption_The_Heart_of_the_Gospel, December 3, 2009.

John Piper, "Visiting Orphans in a World of Aids and Abortion" [sermon online]; available from www.desiringgod.org/ResourceLibrary/Sermons/ByDate/1999/1067_Visiting_Orphans_in_a_World_of_AIDS_and_Abortion, November 17, 2009.

John Piper, "Adoption Is Greater Than the Universe" [video online]; available from www.desiringgod.org/Blog/1113_Adoption_Is_Greater_than_the_Universe, November 17, 2009.

John Piper, "What Is Your Stance on Married Couples Using Birth Control Pills?"www.desiringgod.org/ResourceLibrary/AskPastorJohn/ByDate/4432_What_is_your_stance_on_married_couples_using_birth_control_pills, January 27, 2010.

TheResurgence, "Interview with John Piper," http://theresurgence.com/interview_with_john_piper_audio, January 25, 2010.

Noël Piper's Blog, http://noelpiper.com/2009/10/31/orphan-sunday-118-something-that, January 25, 2010.

Desiring God, "A Letter to Noël Saying Yes to Adoption" www.desiringgod.org/ResourceLibrary/TasteAndSee/ByDate/1995/4335_A_Letter_to_Nol_Saying_Yes_to_Adoption, January 25, 2010.

Saddleback Web cast www.saddleback.com/webcast/civilforum/orphansandadoption.

David Platt, *Radical: Taking Back Your Faith from the American Dream* (Colorado Springs: Multnomah, 2010).

The Church at Brook Hills, "Care for Children" www.brookhills.org/local/adults/care-for-children.html, January 27, 2010.

International Justice Mission, "Injustice Today" www.ijm.org/ourwork/injusticetoday, January 4, 2011.

EBook
Ed Keller and Jon Berry, *The Influentials* (New York: Free Press, 2003).

Majorie Howard, "Constantly Caring: Ukrainian student creates program to help orphans in her native city," *Tufts Journal,* http://tuftsjournal.tufts.edu/archive/2008/january/corner/index.shtml, March 10, 2010.

Mark Russell, *The Missional Entrepreneur: Principles and Practices for Business as Mission* (Birmingham, AL: New Hope Publishers, 2010).

Tom Davis, *Fields of the Fatherless* (Colorado Springs, CO: David C. Cook, 2008), 33.

Andreas J. Kostenberger, *God, Marriage, and Family* (Wheaton: Crossway, 2004), 132.

Douglas Moo, "The Letter of James" in *The Pillar New Testament Commentary* (Grand Rapids: Eerdmans, 2000), 97.

J. I. Packer, *Knowing God* (Downers Grove: InterVarsity, 1973), 206–207.

Aristides, "The Apology of Aristides the Philosopher." Translated from the Syriac Version by D. M. Kay, www.earlychristianwritings.com/text/aristides-kay.html, November 17, 2009. Emphasis added.

See Arnold Dallimore, *George Whitefield*, Vol. 2 (Carlisle: Banner of Truth, 2004, reprint), 274; 441-453. Quoted in Arnold Dallimore, *Spurgeon: A New Biography* (Carlisle: Banner of Truth, 2005, reprint), 126.

Janet and Geoff Benge, *George Muller* (Seattle: YWAM, 1999), 119. For a further outworking of the relationship between God's adoption of us and our adoption of children see Russell Moore's *Adopted for Life* (Wheaton: Crossway, 2009).

Tony Merida, *Faithful Preaching* (Nashville: Broadman Press, 2009).

Ron Ruthruff, *The Least of These: Lessons I Learned from Kids on the Street* (Birmingham, AL: New Hope Publishers, 2010).

Woman's Missionary Union, www.wmu.com,
    Project HELP (Fighting Human Exploitation)
    WORLDCRAFTS (Fair Trade ministry)

CHAPTER 1

Tom Davis—http://blog.beliefnet.com/redletters/
Red Letters is the official blog of Children's HopeChest founder, president, and CEO, Tom Davis.

Children's Hopechest—www.hopechest.org/
Children's HopeChest believes that every orphan has the right to know God, experience the blessing of family, and have the opportunity to develop independent living skills.

CHAPTER 4

Russell D. Moore
www.russellmoore.com/
Moore to the Point is the blog of Russell D. Moore, author of Adopted for Life. Moore serves as senior vice-president for academics and dean of the School of Theology at the Southern Baptist Theological Seminary in Louisville, Kentucky.

Christian Alliance for Orphans
www.christianalliancefororphans.org/
The Christian Alliance for Orphans unites more than 80 respected Christian organizations and a national network of churches. Working together, our joint initiatives *inspire, equip*, and *connect* Christians to "defend the cause of the fatherless" in adoption, foster care, and global orphan care.

Orphan Sunday
www.orphansunday.org
The Orphan Sunday campaign is led by the Christian Alliance for

Orphan, a national coalition of organizations and churches committed to the gospel and the orphan. More than 1,000 churches held Orphan Sunday events in 2009.

Desiring God
www.desiringgod.com
One pastor who has set an incredible example is Dr. John Piper. If one were to do a search for adoption on Dr. Piper's ministry Web site, www.desiringgod.org, you would find about 37 pages of resources such as sermons, letters, blog posts, and more about God's adoption of us and our role to reflect God's mercy.

God's Heart for the Orphan
www.saddleback.com/aboutsaddleback/signatureministries/orphancare
God's Heart for the Orphan is the orphan-care ministry of Saddleback Church.

The Church at Brook Hills
www.brookhills.org
The Church at Brook Hills has numerous sermons and other resources devoted to the subject of adoption, orphan care, and serving the community through local disciple making.

International Justice Mission
www.ijm.org
International Justice Mission is a human rights agency that secures justice for victims of slavery, sexual exploitation, and other forms of violent oppression.

World Orphans
www.worldorphans.org
World Orphans is committed to rescuing millions of orphaned and abandoned children, strengthening the indigenous church, and impacting communities with the gospel of Jesus Christ through church-based orphan prevention, rescue, care, and transition programs in the least reached areas of the world.

Journey 117

www.journey117.org

Journey117 is a ministry of World Orphans that exists to equip influential orphan advocates through high impact Journey trips that offer informative teaching, practical experiences to serve cross culturally, and training to impact your personal advocacy for the sake of the orphan and widow.

CHAPTER 5

Homes of Hope for Children

www.hohfc.org/

The mission of Homes of Hope for Children is to serve children in crisis throughout Mississippi by providing strong, Christian homes to every child that lives on the Homes of Hope campus while ensuring that each child is loved unconditionally and has their physical, spiritual, and emotional needs met.

HopeHouse International

www.hopehouseinternational.org/

HopeHouse exists so that orphans can become adopted...by assisting Ukrainian Christian couples with adequate housing thus making the adoption of orphans possible.

KievKonnect

www.kievkonnect.com

The Church Planting Program of the Kiev Theological Seminary, under the direction of Joel and Mary Ellen Ragains, trains and equips church planters to plant reproducible churches in Ukraine and throughout the former Soviet Union.

Lifesong for Orphans

www.lifesongfororphans.org

Lifesong for Orphans seeks to mobilize the church, His body, where each member can provide a unique and special service: some to adopt, some to care, some to give. This mission is accomplished through a variety of ministries involve Orphan Care and Adoption Grants and Loans. Currently, Lifesong for Orphans has projects in Ethiopia, Honduras, Liberia, Zambia, India, and Zambia.

CHAPTER 6

Adoption Discovery
www.adoptiondiscovery.org/
Adoption Discovery is a seven-week small group that walks potential adoptive parents through the adoption process, helping them to better understand the process and helping them to be educated consumers.

Abba Fund
www.abbafund.org/
The Abba Fund provides interest-free loans and matching grants for Christian families to help with the up-front costs associated with adoptions. Abba Fund also can assist churches in establishing and managing an adoption fund.

Tapestry/Irving Bible Church
tapestry.irvingbible.org
Tapestry is the adoption and foster-care ministry of Irving Bible Church. Tapestry is considered by most the orphan care community as an exemplary church-based ministry to adoptive and foster families.

SBC Adoption Fund for Ministers
www.sbcadoption.com
The Adoption Fund for Ministers exists to assist Southern Baptist ministers financially in the adoption process. The vision is to help ministers bring their children home and ignite a culture of adoption in churches across the country. Introduced at the 2010 SBC Pastor's Conference, this fund is created to help Southern Baptist ministers and missionaries meet the financial burden of adoption.

Bethany Children's Services

www.bethany.org

Bethany Christian Services, the nation's largest adoption agency, also cares for women facing unplanned pregnancies and orphans living on five continents. Bethany's comprehensive services include adoption, temporary foster care, counseling, training, and family support because children thrive in safe, loving, and strong families. Bethany is committed to finding the best families for children in need around the world by demonstrating the love and compassion of Jesus Christ.

CHAPTER 8

Reach Orphans with Hope

www.reachorphanswithhope.org

Reach Orphans with Hope is a nonprofit organization with volunteers committed to help provide financial, emotional, educational, and medical assistance to orphans around the world.

Promise 139

www.promise139.org

Promise 139 is a nonprofit organization in Southern Mississippi formed by people that are passionate in helping orphaned children. This organization consists of adoptive parents and others concerned with the well-being of the fatherless. Our mission is to reach out to the fatherless and make a difference in their future. Promise 139 exists to provide a cultural exchange for underprivileged orphans living in foreign countries.

147MillionOrphans

www.147millionorphans.com

Started by two adoptive moms, 147millionorphans exists to help as many people as possible see the world's 147 million orphans since they have no voice of their own. The wonderful selection of products at 147millionorphans goes to support fatherless children in a variety of ways throughout the world.

"Pure and genuine religion in the sight of God the Father means caring for orphans."
- James 1:27 (NLT)

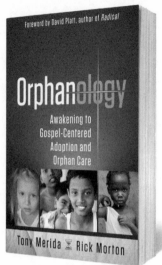

Orphanology unveils the grassroots movement that's engaged in a comprehensive response to serve hundreds of millions of orphans and "functionally parentless" children. You'll see a breadth of ways to care with biblical perspective and reasons why we must.

Heartwarming, personal stories and vivid illustrations from a growing network of families, churches, and organizations that cross culture show how to respond to God's mandate.

Find more information at www.orphanologybook.com

 NEW HOPE
PUBLISHERS

Orphanology: The Bible Study

Powerful truths to share with your church, Sunday school class, or small group.

- Six Bible study lessons correspond to the book chapters of *Orphanology*
- Each lesson includes commentary, teaching plans, discussion questions and more
- Designed to challenge believers to gain insight to help orphans in numerous ways

Order at www.lifebiblestudy.com/orphanology or call 877.265.1605

New Hope® Publishers is a division of WMU®, an international organization that challenges Christian believers to understand and be radically involved in God's mission. For more information about WMU, go to www.wmu.com. More information about New Hope books may be found at www. newhopepublishers.com. New Hope books may be purchased at your local bookstore.

Use the QR reader on your
smartphone to visit us online at
www.newhopepublishers.com

If you've been blessed by this book, we would like to hear your story. The publisher and author welcome your comments and suggestions at: newhopereader@wmu.org.

Missional Living Resources from
NewHopeDigital.com

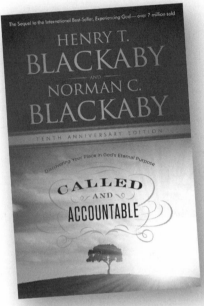

Called and Accountable
*Discovering Your Place
in God's Eternal Purpose*
10th Anniversary Edition
Henry T. Blackaby and
Norman C. Blackaby
1-59669-352-5
978-1-59669-352-4

Compelled
Living the Mission of God
Ed Stetzer and Philip Nation
1-59669-351-7
978-1-59669-351-7

The Deliverer
Kathi Macias
1-59669-308-8
978-1-59669-308-1

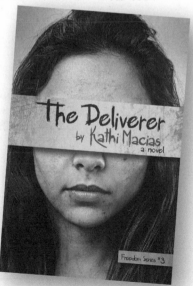

NEW HOPE
P U B L I S H E R S
Gospel-Centered. Missions-Driven.

Available in bookstores everywhere.

For information about these books or any New Hope product,
visit www.newhopepublishers.com.